NEW JERSEY'S REVOLUTIONARY RIVALRY

The Untold Story of Colonel Tye & Captain Huddy

RICK GEFFKEN

THE History PRESS

Published by The History Press
An imprint of Arcadia Publishing
Charleston, SC
www.historypress.com

First published 2025

Manufactured in the United States

ISBN 9781467157506

Library of Congress Control Number: 2025943932

For Dylan, Kate and Ian,

who write their own beautiful histories every day

CONTENTS

FOREWORD

When I thought about the American Revolution before serving as Monmouth County Archivist from 1994 to 2019, my naive concept was that, in a nutshell, the Declaration of Independence was followed by a series of major battles that ended with the Patriot victory at Yorktown. One of my key staff members, the late Mary Ann Kiernan, who served as archival reference specialist, soon enlightened me that, during the conflict, Monmouth, which then included what is now Ocean County, was the site of a bloody civil war between the county's Patriots and Loyalists, exacerbated by raiding parties from Sandy Hook consisting of escaped slaves and Loyalist Refugees. From reading a detailed account in Franklin Ellis, History of Monmouth County (1885), I became aware that Captain Joshua Huddy, a militiaman who lived in what is now Colts Neck, was not only a local hero but also that through his controversial death, he became well known on both sides of the Atlantic before the Treaty of Paris was signed on September 3, 1783, ending the war. The Ellis book, probably written by a group of writers, certainly caught my attention when it claimed, "The name of Captain Joshua Huddy is the most historic of all in the list of Monmouth County patriots who suffered martyrdom in the cause of liberty in the war of the Revolution."

The accounts of Huddy's activities during the war were dramatic, but were they embellished by Ellis and his successors? Was Huddy just an innocent militiaman chosen to die to exact revenge for the death of a Loyalist, Philip White, as indicated by a note pinned to Huddy's corpse? Interest in taking a closer look at Huddy increased with the bicentennial, and in 1978, Donald F.X. Finn compiled a list of Huddy-related materials. When the Monmouth County Archives began mounting annual history exhibits with themes approved by County Clerk M. Claire French, one of the first, held in 2004, was "The Joshua Huddy Era: Documents of the American Revolution." The objective was to gather together primary sources so that historians and others could separate fact from fiction. That exhibit and its catalogue, for which summer employee Shane Wilson, a gifted teenager and future Harvard student and Rhodes Scholar, did much of the work, featured copies of nearly three dozen original documents about Huddy. What emerged was that while Huddy was undoubtedly a man of extraordinary courage who survived narrow escapes in the cause of revolution, he also had a troubled past, including dissolute behavior that prompted his expulsion from the Quakers in Salem County, where he lived before moving to Monmouth. In Monmouth, he continued to draw attention for his antisocial acts that sometimes resulted in court cases. Huddy was a fascinating, complex character whose murder ensnared George Washington in a difficult dilemma.

To weave a cohesive, readable narrative out of the many threads connected to Joshua Huddy is a challenging task that only a skilled storyteller like Rick Geffken can achieve. Geffken's research far exceeded the resources in the 2004 catalogue. Going beyond recent studies by scholars such as Michael Adelberg, James J. Gigantino and Graham R. Hodges, Geffken uncovered more information about Huddy's early life and crafted a much more nuanced view of Titus, known as Colonel Tye. Titus, the biracial son of a Loyalist and one of his enslaved women, escaped his master and led the raiders who attacked Huddy's home and temporarily captured him. Titus may have died as a result of a gunshot wound inflicted that day by Huddy; irrevocably connected, they are the chief protagonists of Geffken's history. Geffken, whose previous research and writing, notably *Stories of Slavery in New Jersey* (2021), has shed much light on African American bondage in the Garden State, elucidates Titus's background and point of view.

For Huddy's contemporaries, how one viewed the Huddy affair depended to a considerable extent on one's own allegiances. The ardent Loyalists, whose property had been confiscated by the Patriots, clearly saw Huddy as a dangerous enemy who had boasted about lynching one of their men. For their part, the Patriots viewed Huddy as a hero: a courageous veteran of numerous battles and skirmishes who had managed to escape death on more than one occasion and who, according to Loyalist reports, met his demise calmly and bravely, dictating his will and shaking hands with his chief executioner, Richard Lippincott. Huddy's popularity is shown by the public outcry after his lynching, the way his body was brought ceremoniously from Highlands all the way to Freehold and the petition with hundreds of signatures sent to George Washington demanding justice.

Geffken features the important role of women in the Huddy story, including but not limited to Huddy's two wives, his servant Lucretia Emmons and the mothers of Titus and Asgill. He also provides an updated account of the rescue from execution of a British officer, Captain Charles Asgill. Asgill was selected by orders of General Washington unless the British turned over Lippincott, who was following orders of former New Jersey Governor William Franklin, certainly one of the chief villains in this tangled web of interrelationships.

Huddy's death on April 12, 1782, was an outrage, especially since it came after the war was, except for the peace treaty, essentially over. Washington's unsuccessful demands to British General Clinton to deliver Lippincott and his determination to execute the unlucky Asgill almost derailed the peace talks and became an international incident that, fortunately, was resolved through diplomacy and his mother's love.

With a focus on Huddy and Titus, together with a supporting cast of sixty-nine other "Principal Characters" identified at the beginning of his book, Geffken provides a far different picture of the American Revolution than merely a series of battles. He helps us understand the impact of the war on individuals on opposing sides, often former neighbors, who lived and sometimes died during the conflict, providing the reader with insights on what it would have been like to witness tumultuous Monmouth County during those violent years.

—GARY D. SARETZKY

ACKNOWLEDGEMENTS

Thank you to these people for their suggestions and help along my way: Kim Bedetti, Maggie Beekman, Alice Berman, Michele Donnelly, Shannon Eadon, Andrew Feldman, Maureen Foster, Claire Garland, Janis Gibson, Gloria and Charlie Gross, Walter Guenther, Christine Giordano-Hanlon, Doug Hart, Dana Howell, Mary Hussey, Jo-Anne Olszewski, Bernadette Rogoff, Jan Rohn, Steve Ross, John Schneider, George Severini, Jessica Solomon, Charlie Swerdlow, Teresa Vega, Joe Zemla and others. I continue to be inspired by Michael Adelberg and Graham Russell Gao Hodges. To those I may have left off my gratitude list, mea culpa.

The members and staff of many historical societies and local governments generously opened their archives to me. I thank all the folks at the Daughters of the American Revolution, Great Bridge (VA) Battlefield & Waterways History Foundation, Middletown Historical Society, Monmouth County Archives, Monmouth County Clerk's Office, Monmouth County Historical Association, Navesink Maritime Heritage Association, Ocean County Historical Society, Salem County Clerk's Office, Salem County Historical Society, Sandy Hook Foundation and Shrewsbury Historical Society.

Anne Ammundsen's research and kind personal correspondences about what occurred to her ancestor Charles Asgill in 1782 helped me enormously.

Special thanks to Steve Schreiber for allowing me to include his painting of the HMS *Britannia*, which was commissioned by John Barrows for his Monmouth Timeline (https://monmouthtimeline.org).

I am especially grateful to Gary Saretzky, whom I met when he served as the Monmouth County archivist. His dedication to sharing his knowledge of our county, and more, has long benefited those who love our rich history. Thank you, Gary.

INTRODUCTION

This is the story of two freedom fighters, a true tale of bravery and misfortune, of loyalty and illegality and, ultimately, of revolution and redemption.

Colonel Tye and Captain Huddy could hardly have presented differently—a Black runaway slave versus a white rebellious Patriot. Yet they recognized similarly strong qualities in each other: commitment to cause, nonconformity, fearlessness and conspicuous bravery. Tye and Huddy rubbed against the grain of military traditions of teamwork. Individual freedom was their common lodestar. They were outsiders working within opposing systems, propelled by strong personal drives and dreams.

Neither man lived to see the end of the war they fought—Tye died in action and Huddy was murdered. They died in unusual circumstances, were initially lauded and then forgotten for decades. In their own ways, each fought for life, liberty and the pursuit of happiness. Their head-to-head confrontations foreshadowed the America to come, Black struggle against white domination.

I grew up in Huddy and Tye country. During my lucky summers at Gravelly Point in Highlands, my friends and I would hang out in Huddy Park and sometimes sit on a monument facing Water Witch Avenue. I read the inscription on that stone many times in the 1950s but didn't know that it was yards away from where the Patriot died. His Revolutionary importance wouldn't become clear to me for decades.

The author (on bike) at Gravelly Point, 1954. *Mary Geffken.*

While I researched this book, many wonderful memories resurfaced for the adventuresome boy who rowed across the Shrewsbury River to explore the beaches of Spermaceti Cove and fished near the Sandy Hook Lighthouse. Nostalgia, a sly mistress, seduced me into imagining that I was chosen to author this story. It's a fun thought, but I don't believe the universe works that way.

Still, I was delighted to recognize so many locales associated with the militia captain and his Loyalist foes during the Revolutionary War. During the 1950s, my friends and I would sometimes leave our bungalows on early mornings to go on day-long bicycle trips, pedaling through places Huddy and Tye knew in their time. Billy, Paul, Mike and I would ride carefree through Buttermilk Valley, over Clay Pit Creek to the Oceanic Bridge, cross the Navesink and head east on Rumson Road to Jumping Point. We'd pedal north along Sea Bright's Ocean Avenue with Rocky Point at Hartshorne's Woods to our left. The last leg of our journey was above the Shrewsbury via the Million Dollar Bridge, past Bahrs on Bay Avenue for the home stretch to Gravelly Point.

My life was coincidentally connected again to Huddy and Tye when I was married at a small Rumson church, built on farm property where Tye had been born enslaved.

Depicting the lives of people who lived 250 years ago, especially men who didn't write about themselves, is challenging. I can't know the feelings of an enslaved Black man who self-emancipated and re-created himself into a formidable person of consequence. My attempts to understand Titus/Tye may strike some as audacious overreach. I've tried to be empathetic and fair in my portrayal.

As I looked at Joshua Huddy's complexities, I saw that his personal drives were sometimes contrary to his heroic image. I've no doubt that he was courageous and steadfast in his devotion to the cause of liberty.

In a period of great social inequality, Huddy and Tye fought for different versions of independence and held disparate views of freedom. Their wartime experiences with brutality, confusion and compassion were unfortunately familiar. I hope readers will come away with admiration for both these men.

TERMINOLOGY

Throughout the text, I use the terms *slave*, *chattel slave* or *enslaved person* somewhat interchangeably. Likewise *slaveholder*, *slave master* or *enslaver*. I employ these descriptives as they were used in the eighteenth century or to avoid repetition that might distract the reader. Black friends and scholars who study the history of chattel enslavement use "enslaved person" these days because it correctly emphasizes and dignifies the person's humanity. "Slave" sounds like it was a person's occupation or a job. People owned by someone else did not choose what to do, nor were they paid by their owners.

There are several ways to describe the people on opposing sides in the American Revolution. Patriots sometimes called themselves "Whigs." The British called them "rebels" and worse. I trust that whichever names I employ are clear within the context.

PRINCIPAL CHARACTERS

COLONEL TYE (1754–1780), aka Titus, runaway enslaved to John Corlies
HUDDY, JOSHUA (1735–1782), aka Jack Huddy, rebel militiaman hanged by British at Sandy Hook

AKIN, ABIEL (1732–1809), judge of Freehold Admiralty Court
ANTOINETTE, MARIE (1755–1793), queen of France, wife of Louis XVI
APPLEGATE, CATHERINE (1732–1786), wife of Levi Hart; second wife of Joshua Huddy
APPLEGATE, HANNAH (1740–1786), sister of Catherine Applegate, wife of Jonas Solomon
APPLEGATE, JACOB (1689–1768), Middletown farmer
ASGILL, SIR CHARLES (1714–1788), 1st Baronet, father of Captain Charles Asgill
ASGILL, CHARLES (1763–1823), British captain and POW chosen to die in revenge for Joshua Huddy execution
ASGILL, SARAH (1729–1816), née Pratviel, mother of Captain Charles Asgill
CARLETON, SIR GUY (1724–1808), appointed British commander-in-chief 1782
CLINTON, GENERAL SIR HENRY (1730–1795), British general during Revolutionary War
CORLIES, JOHN, SR. (1714–1760), Shrewsbury enslaver
CORLIES, JOHN, JR. (1746–1786), younger son of John Sr. and Zilpha Corlies, enslaver of Titus

CORLIES, ZILPHA (1714–1802), née Wilbur, wife of John Corlies Sr., mother of Samuel and John Jr.
CRIPPS, WHITTON (circa 1739–1796), militiaman, brother-in-law of Joshua Huddy
CUNNINGHAM, WILLIAM (1739–1791), British provost marshal in New York City
DUBOIS, BENJAMIN (1739–1827), Dutch Reformed minister, officiant for Joshua Huddy and Catherine Hart
EDWARDS, STEPHEN (1743–1778), Eatontown Loyalist spy
FORMAN, DAVID (1745–1797), aka "Black David," Monmouth Militia and New Jersey State Troop commander
FORMAN, JONATHAN (1758–1803), militia captain, cousin of David Forman
FRANKLIN, BENJAMIN (1706–1790), American inventor and diplomat
FRANKLIN, WILLIAM TEMPLE, SR. (1731–1813), New Jersey royal governor and estranged son of Benjamin
FRENEAU, PHILIP M. (1753–1832), poet of the American Revolution from Middletown Point (Matawan)
GEORGE III (1738–1820), king of England during the Revolutionary War
GORDON, JAMES (1735–1783), British major and friend of Captain Charles Asgill
GRAVIER, CHARLES (1719–1787), comte de Vergennes, French foreign minister
GREEN, JAMES (1750–1811), militia officer captured by Colonel Tye
HART, JACOB (1759–1816), aka John, son of Levy Hart and Catherine (Applegate)
HART, LEVY (1715–1775), from Norfolk England, New York Jewish merchant, husband of Catherine Applegate
HART, REBECCA (1758–1838), daughter of Levy Hart and Catherine Applegate; stepdaughter of Joshua Huddy
HARTSHORNE, ESEK (1728–1795), Quaker enslaver in Highlands, New Jersey
HAZEN, MOSES (1733–1803), brigadier general in Continental Army
HOWE, RICHARD (1726–1799), British admiral, brother of William
HOWE, GENERAL WILLIAM (1729–1814), British commander-in-chief, brother of Richard
LAWRENCE, ELISHA (1740–1811), Loyalist colonel from Upper Freehold, New Jersey
LIPPINCOTT, RICHARD (1745–1826), British captain who executed Joshua Huddy

Livingston, William (1723–1790), governor of New Jersey
Longstreet, Captain Elias (1747–1888), husband of Rebecca Hart (1758–1838); British POW
Longstreet, John (1712–1804), Freehold attorney and court justice
Louis XVI (1754–1793), king of France
Moody, James (1744–1809), Loyalist lieutenant from Little Egg Harbor
Morris, Colonel Lewis (1601–1691), plantation owner from Wales, Barbados and Tinton Falls
Morris, Lewis (1671–1746), nephew and heir of Colonel Lewis Morris
Murray, Joseph (1720–1780), Middletown militiaman murdered by Loyalists
Murray Hyde, Mary Crawford (1855–1936), historian, great-granddaughter of Joseph Murry
North, John (?), captor of Philip White
Paine, Thomas (1737–1809), philosopher author of *The American Crisis*
Piatt, Martha (1766–1842), née Huddy, daughter of Joshua Huddy
Randolph, Benjamin (1738–1791), Philadelphia cabinetmaker
Randolph, Daniel (1733–1792), attorney, at Toms River Blockhouse with Joshua Huddy
Randolph, James (1730–1781), Toms River entrepreneur, privateer partner of Joshua Huddy
Russell, John, Jr. (1755–1826), Shrewsbury rebel involved in the killing of Philip White
Sarah (circa 1735–circa 1805), owned by Corlies family, enslaved mother of Titus/Tye
Scudder, Nathaniel (1733–1781), Monmouth Militia officer
Shepherd, Elisha (1750–1834), militiaman and POW
Simcoe, John Graves (1752–1806), British commander of Queen's Rangers
Skinner, Cortlandt (1729–1799), British general, commander of Skinner's Greens
Smock, Barnes (1738–1829), captain, Monmouth Militia, captured by Colonel Tye
Solomon, Jonas (1731–1815), husband of Hannah Applegate (1740–1786)
Solomon, Rebecah (1765–circa 1817), daughter of Jonas Solomon and Hannah Applegate; wife of Elias Longstreet
Taylor, George (1717–1786), Middletown militia officer who defected to British
Tilton, Clayton (1748–1808), one of three Loyalist brothers

Tilton, Ezekiel (1740–1782), one of three Loyalist brothers
Tilton, John (1741–1805), one of three Loyalist brothers
Van Cleef, Elizabeth (1705–1790), wife of William Covenhoven of Freehold
Von Knyphausen, General Wilhelm (1716–1800), Hessian officer on the British side
Washington, George (1732–1799), Continental Army commander, first president of the United States
White, Aaron (1763–1801), from a Shrewsbury Loyalist family
White, Philip (1756–1782), from a Shrewsbury Loyalist family
Woodhull, Reverend John Tennent (1744–1824), Old Tennent Church pastor

Chapter 1

BLACK POINT

From the first hour of the war, he devoted himself to the cause of Liberty.
—William S. Stryker

The return trip along the Old Burlington Path did not go well for the Loyalist Refugees. The unruly cattle slowed them down on the dozen miles from Jewstown to the coast. Most of the stolen cows drowned as they were herded over the shallow streams feeding into the Swimming River. Worse, the clattering march through the woods and bogs alerted the militia to the Loyalists' location. The horse-mounted militiamen chased their withdrawing enemies, harassing them with musket fire. For a while, it looked like they'd overtake the retreating wagons.

The militia shot and killed half a dozen Refugees. A few who were wounded, too weak to continue their flight, became an accidental rear guard, slowing the pursuers just long enough for the main contingent to avoid another set-piece battle.

At Black Point, the bedraggled Loyalists hurriedly boarded the boats left hidden two days before. Pushing off, they rowed toward the far northern end of a spit of land that reached toward New York Harbor. If they could make it to their base camp at the foot of the Sandy Hook Lighthouse, their miseries would be over.

Worn out from the chase, the Refugees relied on adrenaline alone to power straining arms and legs. The rhythmic slapping of oars hitting the summer morning water was answered by the unruly squawking of dozens of laughing gulls.

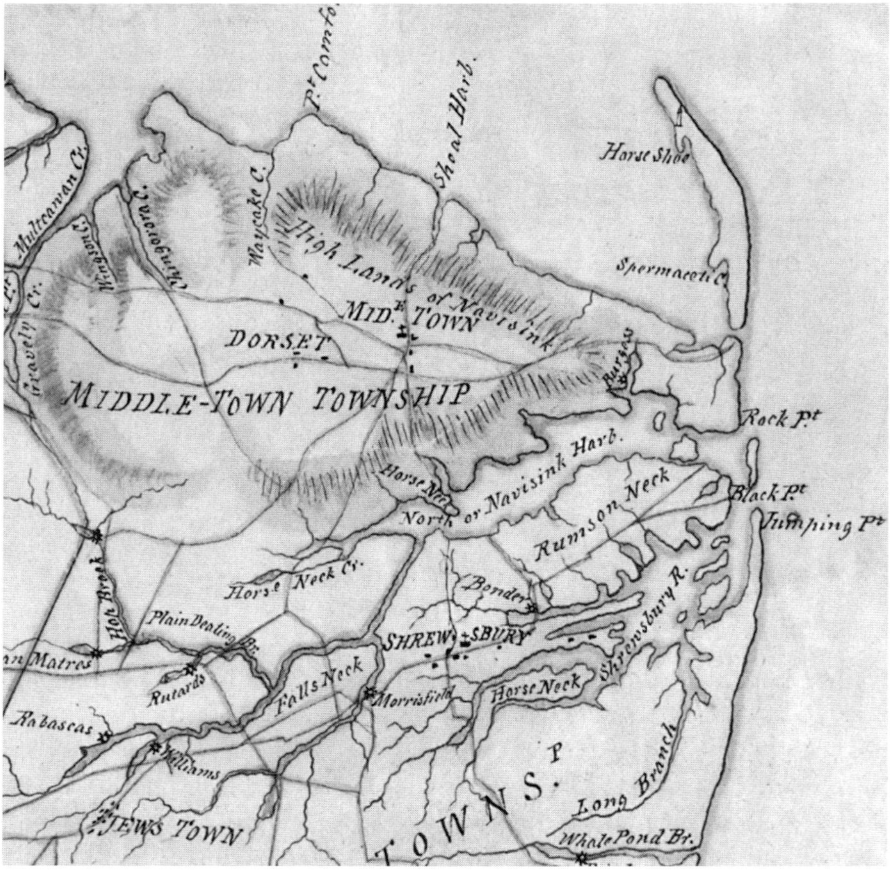

Jewstown (*lower left*), Black Point (*middle right*) and the Sandy Hook Lighthouse (see the icon above "Horse Shoe," *upper right*). *Public domain.*

In the midst of these troops—some civilians, some trained soldiers—one sat grimacing in pain, a bloodstained piece of torn shirt covering his wrist. He had guided this war party to capture a particularly impudent and hated rebel. Nicked during the short siege at the man's house, he was satisfied they'd completed the mission, his throbbing wound be damned.

The six-foot-tall man everyone called "Colonel" wasn't really a commissioned officer. He earned the honorary title for his natural leadership and knowledge of Monmouth County rebel territory. He was a mocha-colored runaway slave who grew up in the area. He escaped only a few years before, when he was twenty years old.

The Colonel and his raiders were widely feared by locals, many of them farmers and slaveholders. They'd never seen armed Black men before the war. The Colonel's emboldened troops had lately launched attacks deeper into the countryside, riding farther and farther inland in pursuit of provisions and vengeance. Local newspaper reports had sneered at the mix of Black and white Loyalist fighters as "a mongrel crew."

As the sun rose over the ocean on this early September morning in 1780, each of the beleaguered oarsmen concentrated on the back of the man in front of him, straining to strike the water in unison. Ahead was a long, six-mile pull to the lighthouse, a 103-foot-tall octagonal tapering stone tower of blazing white. Its signal beacon had guided ships into New York Harbor for fifteen years.

The outgoing tide's swift current worked in the Refugees' favor, making the trip easier, faster. Still, they had to plow through swirling ocean waves and "the Gut," a break in the barrier beach between wild open water and the calmer bay. They'd have a smoother go of it hugging the shoreline between Spermaceti Cove and the Horseshoe. They'd beach their boats close to a rudimentary camp in the shadow of the lighthouse.

Refugeetown on the Hook sheltered dozens of their fellows, Loyalist men and women who were forced to leave their homes and farms by rebellious and hateful neighbors. Dozens of Black men and women who'd been promised freedom for military duty also lived in the shantytown. Some, too old or sickly to fight, remained enslaved to white Refugees.

Near his boat's midsection, the Colonel intentionally faced forward so he could ignore the fading view of the farm he ran from years before. His prisoner, a white militia captain, stared in the opposite direction past his captor, whom he considered "a mulatto." The captain anxiously scanned the shoreline they left behind, hoping for rescue. He was furious at himself for the complacency that had him at the mercy of these rogues. Despite his usually cautious instincts, he'd let his personal guards visit their families the night before. He slept unprotected at home for one night. "Fool," he thought, "you damned fool!"

Four boats were halfway across the narrow part of the Shrewsbury River when the lull of lapping waves was interrupted by the high-pitched staccato of musket balls zipping left and right. Several men winced at the sharp stings of lead balls ripping into their arms and sides. A few died instantly. In shock and confusion, they ducked below the gunwales or fell overboard. Amid capsized boats, splintered oars and floating equipment, flailing men screamed and fought the tide and one another. Panicked, a half dozen drowned.

The captive, Joshua Huddy, took a hit to his thigh. He flipped into the warm, fast-flowing water, kicking his way as best he could despite searing pain. He struggled back toward Black Point, diving occasionally as his rescuers kept firing over him, around him and, to his horror, at him.

The Black leader, Colonel Tye, was also desperate to get to dry land. He half-paddled with one good arm, his immobile right wrist no help. He swallowed more salt water than air.

Chapter 2

HUDDYS OF BURLINGTON AND SALEM

True godliness does not turn men out of the world,
but enables them to live better in it and excites their endeavors to mend it.
—*William Penn*

Hugh Huddy arrived in West Jersey around the turn of the eighteenth century from Cornwall, part of the great wave of English immigrants. Many of these newcomers were Quakers, attracted by William Penn's plans for spiritually based colonies on both sides of the Delaware River. Huddy stopped briefly at Salem before settling farther upriver at a place originally called New Beverly. He married Martha Hunlock in a Quaker ceremony at the renamed Burlington in May 1701. Hugh Huddy's commitment to the Society of Friends would soon be shaken by a Quaker apostate.

New Jersey surveyor George Keith believed that Quakers had strayed too far from orthodox Christianity. He also found more favorable advancement opportunities within the Church of England. Visiting Burlington in 1702, Keith proselytized for the Church's Society for the Propagation of the Gospel in Foreign Parts. Hugh Huddy and other "Keithians" were founders of the Episcopal Church of St. Mary.

As one of Burlington's most prominent Anglicans, Hugh Huddy garnered influential appointments in English West Jersey. He became a postmaster, lieutenant colonel in the New Jersey Militia, high sheriff, attorney and judge—and also a member of Governor Robert Hunter's New Jersey Council. Queen Anne of England granted him a fourteen-year monopoly in 1706

Between three & fore of the Clock In ye Afternoone 1742/3

Hannah White Daughter of John White By
Elizabeth his wife was Born ye 27 of ye 5 mo: 1735

Mary White Daughter of John White By
Elizabeth his wife was Born ye 9 of ye 12th mo: 1739

Joshua Huddy Son of Daniel Huddy By Elizabeth
his wife was Born the 8th day of ye 11th mo: 1735

Top: Hugh Huddy's stage wagon service connected the colonial New Jersey capitals of Burlington and Perth Amboy. *Philadelphia Museum of Art.*

Bottom: March was the first month of the Quaker calendar year, so Joshua Huddy was born on January 8, 1735 (last two lines of birth record). *Quaker Records, via Ancestry.com.*

for the first chartered "stage-wagon" service in America. The Burlington to Perth Amboy Stagecoach Line carried passengers on the bumpy fifty-mile journey along an ancient Lenape trail between the West and East Jersey capitals of Burlington and Perth Amboy.

Hugh and Martha Huddy's son Daniel married Elizabeth White in Burlington in 1732. With money from his inheritance, Daniel bought a small Salem farm a decade later. A saddler by trade, Daniel Huddy applied to Salem's Society of Friends for "good-standing," the Quaker designation for people wed at another meeting. The Salem Meeting was simply following the strict provision of waiting for verification from Burlington before admitting the Huddys.

Jack Huddy

Daniel and Elizabeth Huddy arrived in Salem with a six-year-old son they called Jack. Baptized Joshua, the boy would grow up to be as strong and courageous as his biblical namesake, although Jack Huddy often tumbled walls down on himself in later life.

Nestled between its eponymous river and Fenwick Creek in an isolated part of southwestern New Jersey, Salem was a busy commercial port. The town dock was frantic, with hundreds of boats connecting it to a growing profusion of communities up and down the Delaware River.

Life on the lower Delaware was far from idyllic, but it was usually predictable. A boy growing up in a small riverfront town during the mid-eighteenth century was expected to conform. He had to learn practical farming skills—clearing fields, planting and harvesting crops, caring for horses and livestock, digging wells and mending fences. Throwing a line well and firing a musket accurately were essential for bringing home fish and game animals.

Curious farm boys might sneak away to spend hours wandering Salem's wharfs and docks, watching boat builders and helping fishermen. Stronger teenagers could make some money loading and unloading the skiffs and sloops coming down from Burlington or the Durham boats plying the river trade to and from Philadelphia. Learning to handle small watercraft offered relief from boring farm work for some. A clever boy could become, well, a Jack of many trades, all the while following the faith of his parents.

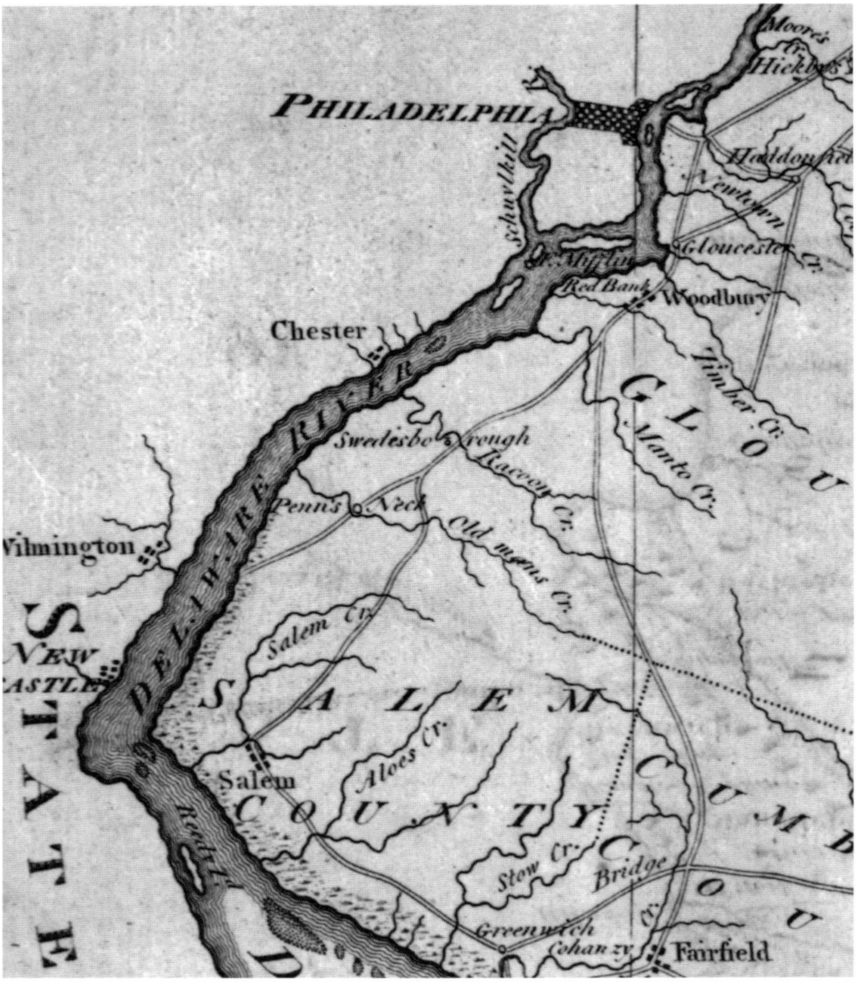

Eighteenth-century Salem, New Jersey. *Library of Congress.*

Salem Quaker Meeting

If by allowing Daniel Huddy to join the Salem Meeting Quaker elders thought that he'd be another compliant contributor to the Society of Friends, their expectations would be upended. Daniel filed multiple complaints against his fellow believers. More than once he demanded "to recover his due"—payments he believed other Quakers owed him for goods or services. Maybe Daniel Huddy saw his grievances through the lens of a core Friends principle—follow your Inner Light. If he did, he misinterpreted its meaning.

Whether or not his father's actions were justifiable, young Jack Huddy absorbed what was modeled for him—make sure you get what's yours. The other Quaker concept, Inner Stillness, eluded both father and son.

Ostracized

Jack Huddy's troubles as he grew up were not private family matters. His Salem neighbors watched as he abandoned his faith, married for money and defrauded family and friends. They saw Jack for what he was, a repeat offender frequently dragged into court and, once, even thrown into jail.

Elizabeth Huddy died in 1755. Within a year, Daniel married the widow Rachel Nicholson. We can't say for certain how these family events affected Jack Huddy, but his problems became public not too long afterward.

In 1756, the Salem Quaker Meeting clerk recorded this about Jack Huddy:

> *Suffered himself to Lead by the Enemy of the Welfair of our Souls Pease and our Present wellbeing into Evil and Loose Company and the Corruption of the world to the Raising Scandalous Reports: and Unchristian Behavior Concerning him; and in stead of Clearing of himself hath Absconded and left the place in a Disorderly manner Contrary to our known and Christian practice.*

His specific violations weren't recorded. Maybe he was drinking hard spirits, gambling on the Sabbath, whoring or fighting. The Salem Quaker elders counseled Jack to modify his behaviors. The resistant twenty-two-year-old Jack Huddy ignored their polite admonitions.

When offered another chance, Jack equated accepting forgiveness with weakness. He refused to accept responsibility for his scandalous actions, simply walking away from his family's faith. As loving and understanding as Quakers always aspired to be, they had their limits. Jack's intransigence got him expelled from, or as Quakers say, "read out of," the Salem Meeting on January 28, 1757:

> *Wee Disown the Said Joshua Huddy as a member of the Society of the People Called Quakers and Testify against him and all his Disorderly Practices untill by a Sincear and harty Repentance gives Reason for his Exceptance again which are our Desires if it may so please the Lord in*

> *mercy to Extend the visitation of Love to bring him to a Sence of his Evil ways and Repentance again.*

Despite the disapproval and shaming by neighbors and friends, Jack obstinately insisted on being his own man. He would carry this angry and distrustful mien his entire life, confronting perceived offenders head on, rarely backing down.

Jack's First Marriage

Following his expulsion from the Quakers, Jack Huddy had several minor run-ins with the law, but his legal troubles escalated seriously after he married Mary Borden in 1764. Not much is known about the widow other than she was a few years older than Huddy. Her deceased husband, name unknown, may have been a Borden, Burden or Bardin, from either Burlington or Monmouth County.

Jack might have felt genuine about Mary, but he also saw her as a lonely woman with an inheritance. A year after their wedding, the usually impoverished Huddy put a down payment on the purchase of a three-hundred-acre plantation at Haynes Neck in Mannington, owned by a James Popino.

Jack Huddy must have used his wife's resources to buy the farm, but he needed more. He borrowed £200 from his sister Hannah and her husband, Whitton Cripps. By the time he was twenty-nine, Jack had figured out how to get and use other people's money, inveigling loans from friends and neighbors whenever he could.

Adamantly resistant to authority of any kind, Jack Huddy was developing other unfortunate tendencies. Maneuvering other people for his own needs, he was unwilling, or unable, to repay his debts. He was called to account so often that his actions became a kind of self-sabotage.

Cascading Legal Problems

If he hoped that marriage and property ownership would make him a respected citizen with a comfortable living, Jack never found that stability.

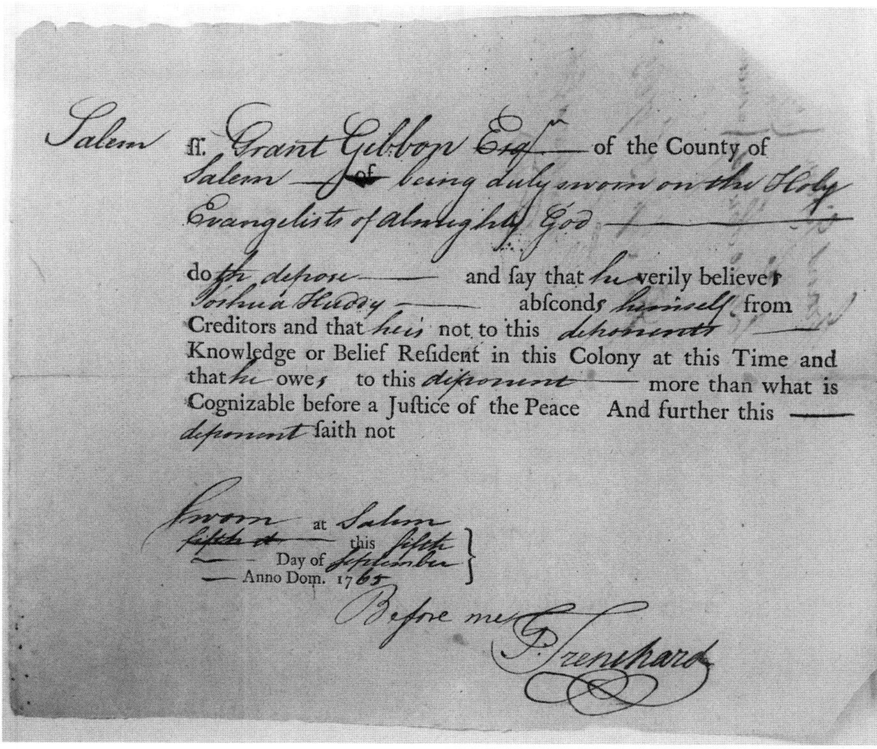

Salem ſſ. Grant Gibbon Esqr of the County of Salem being duly sworn on the Holy Evangelists of Almighty God

doth depose and ſay that he verily believes Joshua Huddy abſconds himself from Creditors and that he is not to this deponents Knowledge or Belief Reſident in this Colony at this Time and that he owes to this deponent more than what is Cognizable before a Juſtice of the Peace And further this deponent ſaith not

Sworn at Salem this fifth Day of September Anno Dom. 1765

Before me P. Trenchard

A 1765 Salem County Court document involving Jack Huddy. *Salem County, New Jersey Clerk.*

He had serious cash flow problems trying to squeeze out meager farm profits. When his creditors came to collect, his stalling and conniving were transparent.

Half a dozen times in as many years, he was sued for defaulting on loans. Sometimes Jack showed up at his Salem County Court hearings. Just as often, his attorneys appeared when he didn't. The sheriff hauled him in to answer charges more than once.

In 1766, Whitton Cripps and his sister Hannah sued Jack Huddy for repayment of their loans. At an August court hearing, the volatile Huddy got into a confrontation with James Popino. Both men were arrested for assault and battery. At the end of the year, the Salem sheriff seized Huddy's farm and put it up for auction.

When the auction and levies on Huddy's goods failed to bring in enough cash to pay what he owed, Huddy was sent to debtors' prison at the Market Street Court House in Salem. We don't know how long he was in jail, but

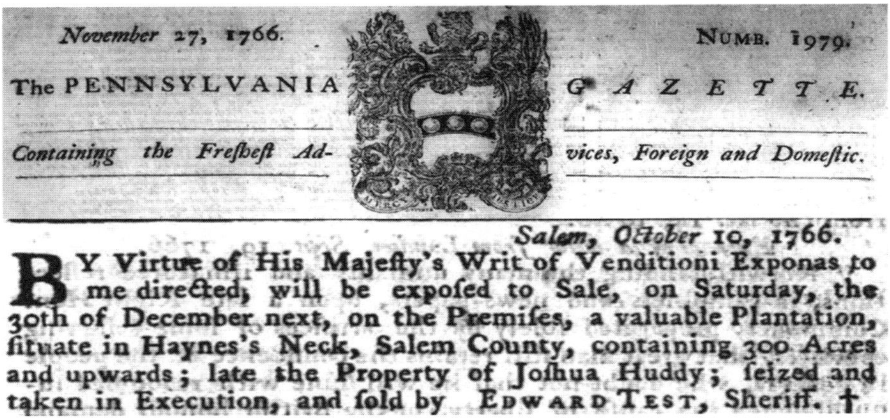

November 27, 1766. NUMB. 1979.

The PENNSYLVANIA GAZETTE.

Containing the Freshest Advices, Foreign and Domestic.

Salem, October 10, 1766.

BY Virtue of His Majesty's Writ of Venditioni Exponas to me directed, will be exposed to Sale, on Saturday, the 30th of December next, on the Premises, a valuable Plantation, situate in Haynes's Neck, Salem County, containing 300 Acres and upwards; late the Property of Joshua Huddy; seized and taken in Execution, and sold by EDWARD TEST, Sheriff. †

The Salem County sheriff seized Joshua Huddy's plantation. *From the* Pennsylvania Gazette.

while being "closely confined" during 1768, Huddy appealed to the New Jersey General Assembly for release, as published in the *Pennsylvania Gazette*:

> *November 27, 1766. Pursuant to an act of the General Assembly of the province of New-Jersey, lately passed, entitled an act for the relief of insolvent debtors; we the subscribers being now closely confined in the county of Salem, and having petitioned the judges of his Majesty's inferior court of common pleas…do give notice to all our creditors, to appear and show cause…before the said judges at the Court-House, in the town of Salem…why we should not be discharged, agreeable to the directions of the said act. Joshua Huddy, Andrew Polson, Abraham Lord, Jacob Harnis.*

Jack Huddy had to start over when he got out of jail. Never cut out to be a yeoman farmer, he tried something else. Court documents during the period describe him as a "Marriner [*sic*]." His innate taste for adventure must have drawn him to try his hand at sailing the trade routes. He navigated small boats between Salem, Burlington and Philadelphia. The last, only a half day's sail upriver, was the major port on the western bank of the Delaware. Jack Huddy charged Salem farmers for shipping their produce to the City of Brotherly Love. He'd return with the proceeds or finished goods they requested, essentials such as clothing, furniture and household items.

While trying to get out of debt, Jack had to literally keep himself above water in the fall of 1771. While sailing home from Philadelphia, Huddy's boat was capsized by a wind gust. The only one of four passengers to

Small sailboat on the Delaware River. *Library of Congress.*

survive, he treaded water for several hours until he was rescued, as noted in the *Pennsylvania Packet*:

> *PHILADELPHIA, October 28, 1771. A few days ago, a small sail boat was overset, by a flaw of wind, on her passage from this city to Salem; by which accident Richard Hacket, Samuel Smith, and a lad were unfortunately drowned. Joshua Hudd, another passenger, after being in the water about three hours, got to shore in a small canoe.*

The incident speaks to Jack's physical prowess as well as his survival instincts. Both would come in handy ten years hence.

During the years Jack Huddy was visiting Philadelphia, the city was rife with developing hostility to its historic Quaker government. Merchants disliked the upper classes controlling the city. The city's rejection of authority made it fertile ground for the revolutionary fervor already brewing in the American colonies. Jack Huddy might have read John Dickinson's "Letters from a Farmer" questioning Britain's colonial polices when it was published in the *Pennsylvania Chronicle*. If he did, it would have appealed to his innate rebelliousness and disenchantment with his Quaker upbringing, perhaps the first stirrings of patriotic feelings.

Huddy's personal setbacks kept piling up during these years, most consequentially the death of his wife, Mary. She was barely forty when she passed away from unknown causes in 1771, leaving Jack alone with two very young daughters. As a man with no instincts for, and less interest in, nurturing children, he turned to relatives for help. He had already burned his bridges with his in-laws, so he might have asked his younger brother's family—Daniel and Agnes Huddy lived in nearby Mannington—to care for his daughters while he worked the river.

The Salem County sheriff was also selling off Huddy's few remaining possessions, chipping away at Jack's diminishing goods and social status. Desperation and loneliness ensnared Huddy in an incident that precipitated his flight from Salem.

Jack Huddy's final live court appearance in Salem occurred in August 1773 when he submitted a confession to a judgement of debt. A much larger problem loomed when he failed to show up for a formal accusation in December. The sheriff couldn't find him. Jack Huddy had disappeared.

Huddy was accused of fornication with a widow named Abigail Smith. While it would barely raise eyebrows today, intimate relations between unmarried people was a crime "against the Form of an Act of the General Assembly of this Province of New Jersey…and against the Peace of our said Lord the King, his Crown and Dignity." The filing was ominously called *Rex vs. Joshua Huddy*.

Apparently, Jack Huddy owed money to Abigail's deceased husband, William Smith. Once again, the opportunistic ne'er-do-well recognized a chance to take advantage of a vulnerable woman. Abigail, executor of her husband's estate, claimed that Huddy seduced her sometime during November, probably while he tried to talk his way out of the debt. The case remained open for almost two years, only dismissed because neither Jack nor Abigail ever appeared at the hearings. His Salem attorneys pursued him for years to recover their fees. Characteristically, Jack had the temerity to countersue them.

Leaving Salem

Huddy found his way to Monmouth County, about to embark on a new path no one in Salem would have predicted, least of all the scofflaw himself. He was going to be swept up in something more to his liking than fathering little girls.

The British American colonies had been stewing for years over home country rule and waves of unfair tariffs. Whatever Jack Huddy's actual feelings about patriotism, his future biographers would give him credit for highly valorous motives. The *Passaic (NJ) Daily Herald* made him out to be a phoenix-like hero:

> *In 1768 Joshua Huddy was practically a penniless man, his property having been seized, and he was in destitute condition. His interest was awakened in the cause of liberty from the very beginning of the struggle with England, and he was eager to defend the rights of the Colonists. After a few years of service in the militia, he was appointed defender of the lives and property of the Colonists in Monmouth County, and enjoyed the reputation of being righteously severe against wrongdoers and of being a most just man.*

Righteous indeed when it came to patriotism, but this "most just man," deservedly lauded for his wartime gallantry, was often a "wrongdoer" in his personal affairs.

Chapter 3

CORLIES OF SHREWSBURY

Corlies was a Quaker, and one of the few in his meeting who refused to free his slaves.
—Crossroads of the American Revolution website

While most Rumson Neck farmers were anticipating another successful harvest as the summer of 1760 dwindled, one Quaker family suffered an unexpected loss. After her husband's death in August, the widow knew that the life they created together for over a quarter of a century would never be the same. Nonetheless, she found comfort in the family they made and the family she owned.

John Corlies's will stipulated that his forty-six-year-old wife, Zilpha, was allowed "the Profits of one third part of all my Houses, Buildings, Land & Meadows…during all the time she remains." The maintenance of the estate fell in large part to the six "Negroes" he left, worth an estimated £220. Her sons, Samuel and John, would keep the farm going more or less as it always had, made easier by the free labor they'd enjoyed for four generations.

Mother

Zilpha and young John inherited four of these people—two men, "a negro wench" named Sarah and her six-year-old, very white-looking son, Titus. Two other slaves were bequeathed to Samuel, married and living on an adjacent farm.

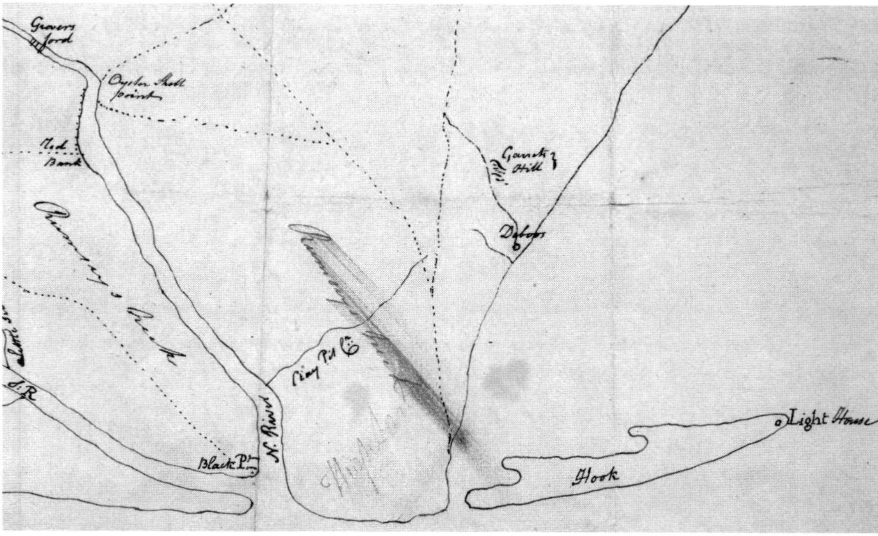

The Corlies family farm was at Black Point (*lower left*) on the Rumson Neck peninsula. *Public domain.*

The Corlies heirs thought of these slaves as property, no different from the furniture or tools left to them. All their neighbors felt the same way. The widespread system of chattel slavery allowed enslavers to use, abuse, buy or sell the people they owned however they wished.

When she ran low on money two years later, Zilpha Corlies confessed to the Shrewsbury Quaker Meeting "that in the time of my distress I did sell a negroe man that did belong to my deceased husband's estate."

Black enslavement came to Monmouth County in 1675, the year Colonel Lewis Morris brought sixty of his enslaved plantation workers from Barbados to Tinton Falls. The Corlies farm was on land Colonel Morris sold to a nephew, a man so brutal that one of his slaves murdered him in 1695.

We know very little about Sarah. Was she born in America, the Caribbean or perhaps Africa? Did a Corlies buy her, or was she the daughter of another of their slaves?

Enslaved Lives

Like all enslaved people in eighteenth-century Monmouth County, Sarah had no say in her own life. She was probably used for the typical farm tasks

Monmouth County Historical Association.

described by historian Graham Hodges: planting potatoes and other root vegetables and harvesting beans, grains, corn and wheat. Small farms of the time usually had at least a few fruit and nut trees, perhaps an apple orchard. She would milk cows and midwife new animals. Sarah's domestic duties might have included cleaning the house, cooking meals, sewing clothes and catering to Zilpha's personal needs. Sarah may have been "rented out" to neighbors who needed extra help from time to time.

As he grew into his mature strength, Titus would mow fields for hay and cut trees for firewood and building material. He'd repair fences and acquire rudimentary carpentry skills, perhaps even some blacksmithing.

Titus would be familiar with cows and horses, tending sheep, goats and chickens and butchering hogs. He'd drive wagons loaded with produce to Corlies's neighbors or local markets. He'd gather the abundant shellfish, clams, oysters and fish from the Navesink and Shrewsbury Rivers. He likely became good at rowing and navigating boats too. Maybe he taught himself to swim. Traveling local roads for two decades, he must have thought about the best routes for escape. Enslaved people were treated as machines whose sole purpose was to make white people's lives easier—and happier.

Although not considered particularly feminine by most enslavers, Black girls and women were sufficiently attractive to lustful white men. This meant that Sarah would submit to the desires of a white man to protect her own life and that of her half-Black, half-white little boy. He was "mulatto"—the obnoxious term derived from the Spanish for mule, an animal born of the mating of a horse and a donkey.

We don't know if Sarah had other children, but if she did, she would have considered her primary responsibility to teach them survival. She modeled how to act around white people with unpredictable prerogatives. She was especially challenged raising the son of the man who violated her.

Slave owners in the eighteenth century often named their mixed children after classical figures, appellations used to distinguish their chattel from traditional "white" names. Titus was very likely named after the first-century Roman military commander (later emperor) who besieged Jerusalem and destroyed the Second Temple. The boy's father would come to regret how fittingly he named his son. (Although some have suggested his name was Titus Cornelius, no primary source document or contemporary report uses that nomenclature.)

Sarah's Titus was born enslaved under the colonial legal doctrine *partus sequitur ventrem* ("that which is born follows the womb"). White men who forced themselves on their enslaved women were not then viewed as rapists as we understand them now. The law gave these men the right to own their mixed children but excused them from any paternal responsibilities. Besides allowing for unrestricted male pleasure, this abhorrent arrangement provided a "natural" increase to their slaveholdings. Few found the common and highly valued white privilege unethical. Even the wives of enslavers didn't care, or pretended not to.

Father

When Titus was born around 1754, Zilpha's husband, John Corlies, was forty. Their son Samuel was eighteen and John Jr. only eight. One of the two older Corlies men must have fathered Titus. So Titus was either John Jr.'s half-brother or his nephew.

It's easy to imagine the two young boys running around the farm playing hopscotch, hoop-rolling and leapfrog. They would look like playmates, but Titus was keenly aware of his inferior status. He was "ordered" when and

Slaves at Middletown's Marlpit Hall slept in the attic accessible by a narrow staircase behind the kitchen hearth. *Monmouth County Historical Association.*

how to play. He didn't share meals with John. He ate lower-quality food and less of it at that. Titus was forced to do the small and large tasks John didn't have to, from fetching water to cleaning out animal stalls. He had to stand by while John punished and mistreated anyone who displeased him.

Corlies slaves lived in a rudimentary dwelling, maybe in a barn alongside cattle and horses. One of the wealthiest families on the Rumson peninsula, the Corlieses wouldn't allow their "servants" inside their living quarters at night. Poorer white people did sometimes sleep under the same roof as their slaves, albeit in different sections of the home. Black families might spend nights in cramped and bare attic spaces, accessible by winding staircases behind the family kitchen hearth, the rising heat providing a little warmth.

Titus grew up learning to ignore what white people called him, the disparaging and belittling names such as "darky," "blacky" and the obvious worst term of all. He observed the Corlies pecking order carefully, not trusting any of them. Titus was especially wary of Samuel Corlies, whose behavior was so erratic that his brother, John, once testified he was "an insane person." Titus was only six when Samuel shot and killed his wife, Lavina, in 1761. At first, Samuel claimed he didn't do it, and then he said his gun went off accidentally. No one needed to tell Titus that these white people were crazy. He had to figure out how to handle yet another personality when John Corlies Jr. married Elizabeth Borden.

Fear and Rage

Titus and Sarah lived with constant apprehension. Neither could defend the other from beatings, lest they suffer the same punishments. By the time he was old enough to understand what was happening when a Corlies man visited his mother at night, Titus was helpless to intercede or protest. Sarah no doubt cautioned him, "Hush now, this is just the way it is." He suppressed his rage and promised himself redress, all the while imagining ways to escape the madness surrounding him.

Even if the meek don't inherit the earth, they sometimes outlive those who do. In 1802, Samuel Corlies Jr. wrote to attorney Richard A. Stockton seeking probate advice on the estate of his grandmother, who had recently died at the age of eighty-eight:

> *Zilpha Corlies, many years before her death, manumitted a Negro woman and a negro man. The woman is very aged and already unable to support herself, and the man, it is probable, before many years will be in the same situation. What steps will be proper for the Executor to take in order to secure their maintenance? Who is to take charge of the old woman? Can the Legatees* [heirs] *forcibly take her out of the hands of the Executor, and dispose of her at their discretion?*

Stockton, named after his father, Richard, a signer of the Declaration of Independence, was himself the executor of Zilpha's will. He informed the heirs that the executor was not responsible for supporting the old woman and that the heirs could "refuse to maintain her unless she is permitted to be with them." This old woman was probably Sarah. The manumitted man is unknown.

Stockton's callous opinion was that, after decades of servitude and service to the Corlies family, Sarah could be abandoned. Whatever the family decided, this was the last known mention of Sarah, mother of Titus.

Chapter 4
THE RUNAWAY

If freedom was the gospel of the abolitionists,
property was the battle cry of the slaveholders.
—Frances D. Pingeon

A constable rode through Shrewsbury Township in the summer of 1771, stopping at homes and farms along his way. He was conducting a survey of people who owned slaves so they could be taxed on their human property. In crude language, counting "All the Neger Slaves & melater, both men and women," he categorized people he viewed as entirely Black and those he saw as mixed, or mulatto. The constable and most white enslavers thought that mixed people were subhuman, belonging to a separate species.

The List

Asher West's final accounting identified fifty-eight individuals who owned ninety-seven people. This was surely an undercount because owners had a good reason to hide property, their chattel slaves, from a nosy local official. Less property meant you owed lower taxes. Perhaps West was offered bribes from friends to record fewer slaves, or maybe he simply believed what the owners told him. We know that West's tally is low because Samuel Corlies, who owned two slaves, did not make the list. We'll never know how many others evaded the tax man.

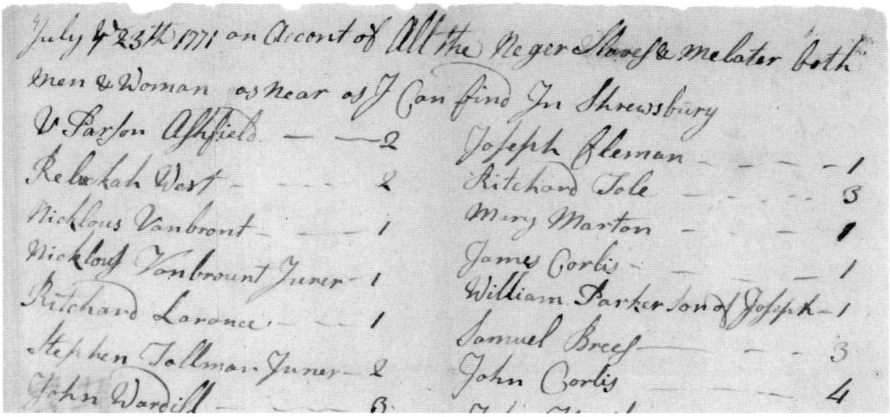

July ye 23th 1771 an Accont of All the Neger Slaves & melater both
men & Woman as near as I Can find In Shrewsbury

V Parson Ashfield — 2
Rebekah West — 2
Nicklous Vanbront — 1
Nicklous Vanbrount Juner — 1
Ritchard Larance — 1
Stephen Tollman Juner — 2
John Wardell — 3

Joseph Fleman — 1
Ritchard Tole — 3
Mary Marton — 1
James Corlis — 1
William Parker son of Joseph — 1
Samuel Breese — 3
John Corlis — 4

A 1771 list of Shrewsbury enslavers with John Corlies Jr. (*lower right*) and his cousin James Corlies (*three lines above*). *Monmouth County Archives.*

The majority of Shrewsbury enslavers owned only one person. Officials from the four other Monmouth County townships—Middletown, Freehold, Dover and Stafford—reported the same trend. The lists have people of different religious observances, including Quakers. The Shrewsbury list included Quaker slaveholders: three Parkers, six Wardells and two Corlies men.

The slaves on the list were just numbers, not important enough to be mentioned by name—except for one man who would become better known than some of the slaveholders themselves.

Zilpha Corlies and her sons, Samuel and John, owned six people. We don't know if these half dozen men and women were the same people bequeathed in her husband John's will a dozen years previously. The family had more slaves than any of their neighbors, one indication of their prosperity. The Corlies defiance of the Shrewsbury Quaker Meeting's admonition against owning slaves was years in the making.

Quaker Intercession

Shrewsbury Quaker elders, as was their practice, made frequent visits to the Corlies farm. As historian Graham Hodges relates, "Quakers did not simply drop by, talk briefly, and then leave. Such conversations could take hours." Their gentle suggestions for reflection, remorse and reform were ignored. John Corlies Sr. was disowned in 1759 for "too much freedom with spirituous liquors." His cousin James was disowned "for departing from our principles," accused of fornication.

On at least three occasions in the late 1760s, the Shrewsbury Meeting accused John Corlies Jr. of violations. Quakers visited to "treat" with him about the accusations of fighting, destroying property and marriage to a non-Quaker woman. The delegations sought John's contrition and written confessions for his misdeeds. For months, Corlies would not acknowledge any wrongdoings. Even after finally admitting some transgressions, he refused to conform to "Good Gospel Order."

Because of nonconformists in their midst, the Shrewsbury Meeting struggled to fully embrace abolition, sometimes offering exceptions to its own rules. The recording secretary reported in 1775 that the meeting was "[c]lear as to [opposing] importing or buying Negros, except one friend who has purchased one that he formerly sold to set him free, which is accordingly done; we believe there is a shortness amongst Friends that have them in educating them in the principles of the Christian Religion." Like many other colonial Americans with contradictory feelings about institutional enslavement, the Shrewsbury Quakers tolerated members who educated their slaves.

When they weren't mere checkmarks, a "negroe Joe" or a "Sally and child" might show up in a last will or a property inventory. If his ownership was disputed, a "negro boy Sam" might appear in a court document. Letters and diaries of white people rarely mention slaves by name—to do so would be to acknowledge their humanity. We would know nothing about the lives of untold numbers of Black people, except for a set of unique sources: hundreds of runaway slave ads published in newspapers.

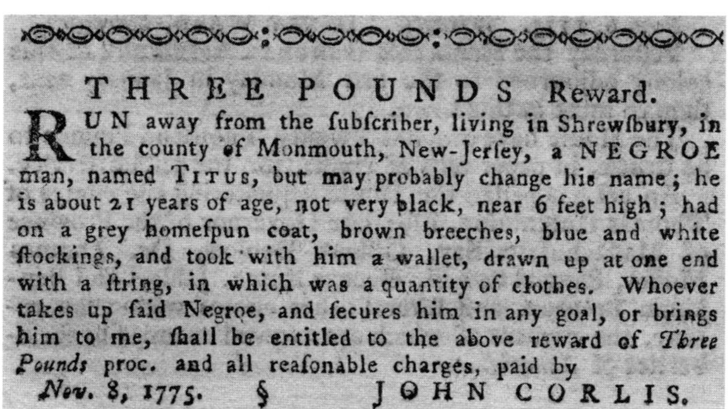

THREE POUNDS Reward.

RUN away from the ſubſcriber, living in Shrewſbury, in the county of Monmouth, New-Jerſey, a NEGROE man, named Titus, but may probably change his name; he is about 21 years of age, not very black, near 6 feet high; had on a grey homeſpun coat, brown breeches, blue and white ſtockings, and took with him a wallet, drawn up at one end with a ſtring, in which was a quantity of clothes. Whoever takes up ſaid Negroe, and ſecures him in any goal, or brings him to me, ſhall be entitled to the above reward of *Three Pounds* proc. and all reaſonable charges, paid by

Nov. 8, 1775. § JOHN CORLIS.

John Corlies Jr.'s ad in the *New York Gazette* and the *Pennsylvania Gazette*. *Via Newspapers.com.*

As important as they are, these ads give us the barest information, tidbits really, about the Black women and men who helped build our country. For all the thousands of runaway slave newspaper ads, we rarely find out what happened to them—were they captured and returned? Were they successful in starting a new life somewhere?

Runaway Reward

John Corlies Jr.'s ad appeared in New York and Philadelphia papers, cities where he suspected his slave might hide. The £3 reward (about $600 today) shows how highly valued Titus was. A grown male slave was worked hard to provide his owner a substantial return on investment, which of course was minimal.

The runaway's physical description—"a NEGROE man, named Titus about 21 years of age…not very black"—suggests a white father and a Black mother.

Runaway ads describing what people wore usually indicate that they left suddenly, taking advantage of the rare opportunities they were unsupervised. But Titus must have planned his escape carefully in advance because he "had on a grey homespun coat, brown breeches, blue and white stockings, and took with him a wallet, drawn up at one end with a string, in which was a quantity of clothes." These details could only have come from someone who knew those plans, his mother. Titus probably confided in her his idea to wait for a cold fall night when the Corlieses were huddled inside by a fire or asleep. When his escape was discovered, John Corlies threatened Sarah with a whipping or worse. She had little choice but to tell him what she knew.

One month before John Corlies's newspaper ad, the Shrewsbury Meeting found "nine of our Members possessed of 24 Negros. One has two, one a man and the other a woman about 22 years old, has misbehaved by having a Melatto Child, proposes freeing her before ye expiration of a year if she behaves well." The meeting also reported on their interactions with the Corlieses:

> *October 1775. We the Committee Appointed by Shrewsbury Monthly Meeting to treat with such Friends belonging to said meeting who are possessed of Slaves, after a friendly conference with said Persons, have agreed with Unanimity to make the following Report, Viz.:*

By His Excellency the Right Honorable JOHN Earl of DUNMORE, His MAJESTY's Lieutenant and Governor General of the Colony and Dominion of VIRGINIA, and Vice Admiral of the ſame.

A PROCLAMATION.

AS I have ever entertained Hopes, that an Accommodation might have taken Place between GREAT-BRITAIN and this Colony, without being compelled by my Duty to this moſt diſagreeable but now abſolutely neceſſary Step, rendered ſo by a Body of armed Men unlawfully aſſembled, firing on His MAJESTY's Tenders, and the formation of an Army, and that Army now on their March to attack His MAJESTY's Troops and deſtroy the well diſpoſed Subjects of this Colony. To defeat ſuch treaſonable Purpoſes, and that all ſuch Traitors, and their Abettors, may be brought to Juſtice, and that the Peace, and good Order of this Colony may be again reſtored, which the ordinary Courſe of the Civil Law is unable to effect; I have thought fit to iſſue this my Proclamation, hereby declaring, that until the aforeſaid good Purpoſes can be obtained, I do in Virtue of the Power and Authority to ME given, by His MAJESTY, determine to execute Martial Law, and cauſe the ſame to be executed throughout this Colony: and to the end that Peace and good Order may the ſooner be reſtored, I do require every Perſon capable of bearing Arms, to reſort to His MAJESTY's STANDARD, or be looked upon as Traitors to His MAJESTY's Crown and Government, and thereby become liable to the Penalty the Law inflicts upon ſuch Offences; ſuch as forfeiture of Life, confiſcation of Lands, &c. &c. And I do hereby further declare all indented Servants, Negroes, or others, (appertaining to Rebels,) free that are able and willing to bear Arms, they joining His MAJESTY's Troops as ſoon as may be, for the more ſpeedily reducing this Colony to a proper Senſe of their Duty, to His MAJESTY's Crown and Dignity. I do further order, and require, all His MAJESTY's Leige Subjects, to retain their Quitrents, or any other Taxes due or that may become due, in their own Cuſtody, till ſuch Time as Peace may be again reſtored to this at preſent moſt unhappy Country, or demanded of them for their former ſalutary Purpoſes, by Officers properly authoriſed to receive the ſame.

GIVEN under my Hand on board the Ship WILLIAM, off NORFOLK, the 7th Day of NOVEMBER, in the SIXTEENTH Year of His MAJESTY's Reign.

DUNMORE.

(GOD ſave the KING.)

> *That we find Zilpha Corlies possessed of two Negroes both females, one aged about fifty, the other thirteen years of age, have no Learning. The old woman she thinks is not fit for Freedom, and don't choose to give Friends any Encouragement in giving the young one her Liberty as directed by the Yearly Meeting but says it should be left to her Direction when the time comes.*
>
> *John Corlies has four Negroes of the male kind whose ages are about Twenty five, Twenty two, Sixteen and Fourteen, they have no learning, and he is not Inclined to give them any, and says he has not seen it his duty to give them their Freedom.*

Enslavers forbid literacy for practical reasons. Reading and writing could enable slaves to conspire against their owners, and pass along secrets such as escape routes and safe houses. Slaveholders lived in constant fear of uprisings and vengeful attacks.

Any hope Titus had for manumission was dashed when he overheard John Corlies resisting the Quaker elders' cautionary advice. Among his objections to their counsel, Corlies said his slaves "have no learning and he is not inclined to give them any." If Titus knew how to read and write, he left us no written documents to prove it. After he left, the Quaker Meeting noted that "John Corlies refuses to manumit his Negros until he sees his own time." They disowned him for "the injustice of keeping our fellow Men in Bondage, but our Labor of Love is rejected by him."

Titus made his decision to run at a most opportune time, though he probably didn't know about the pivotal event affecting his life that had just occurred hundreds of miles south of Shrewsbury. It was the culmination of developments begun in 1771 when the Royal Governor of New York was reassigned to Virgina.

Opposite: Lord Dunmore's 1775 proclamation. *Public domain.*

Chapter 5
THE REFUGEE

I went down to Sandy Hook, toder arternoon.
—George Washington Dixon

During the spring of 1775, reports about the momentous goings-on in Virginia circulated widely throughout the American colonies. The Royal Governor Lord Dunmore, John Murray, took over a Williamsburg arms and ammunition depot, claiming that he had to prepare for a slave insurrection. The militia and citizenry saw his actions as an attempt to disarm them. When a crowd of protestors gathered outside his palace, Dunmore could not abide this public audacity. For years he'd been unhappy about his transfer from Manhattan to this colonial backwater. Now, furious at the lack of respect for royal authority, he threatened to free the slaves of these rebellious citizens in retaliation.

Dunmore's Dilemmas

The distressful news of Dunmore's retribution plan was discussed and debated throughout the colonies, adding fresh kindling to the embers of colonial restlessness. The rumors, half-truths and misinformation about a potentially disastrous action startled everyone, Black and white. Thomas Jefferson called it a "perfect frenzy." Could Virginia, the very place slavery got its misshapen foothold in America, become a place of refuge?

John Murray, Lord Dunmore. *Public domain.*

Dunmore understood the danger to his government at Norfolk. He relocated his headquarters to a fleet a ships in the harbor, his "Floating Town." On November 7, he issued the long-anticipated official document: "I do hereby further declare all indented Servants, Negroes, or others (appertaining to Rebels) free that are willing and able to bear Arms; they joining His Majesty's Troops, as soon as may be, for the more speedily reducing this Colony to a proper Sense of their Duty to His Majesty's Crown and Dignity."

The governor called the several hundred slaves who had already flocked to his side "Dunmore's Ethiopian Regiment." Historian Charles W. Carey offers a more nuanced view: "Most observers consider that Lord Dunmore was the driving force behind the creation of the Ethiopian Regiment…the slaves themselves provided the necessary impetus for bringing about Dunmore's Proclamation of Emancipation…the governor simply responded to slaves' willingness to take up arms in pursuit of liberty."

Dunmore's promises had two broad aims: to increase British fighting forces while simultaneously weakening the rebel economy. Fleeing their masters, dozens of Virginia slaves immediately took off for Williamsburg and Norfolk. Despite all his talk, Dunmore didn't free his own enslaved people.

Estimates of the number of slaves who ran away to the British during the war range between twenty thousand and one hundred thousand. Whatever the actual number, their owners reacted with fury, fighting what they saw as another usurpation of their property rights—how dare these representatives of the home country take their private property! Dunmore was called a "Negro thief," perpetrating a "diabolical scheme." The commonwealth was "hell itself."

Responding to the alarming events in Virginia, Shrewsbury, New Jersey's Committee of Observation ordered both enslaved and free Blacks to surrender their firearms "until the present troubles are settled." It hardly mattered to Titus. He had run away from John Corlies a few days before the news of Dunmore's offer reached New Jersey. Whatever his original plans, once he heard about the proclamation, Titus must have considered the option of going to Virginia.

The Missing Years

We have no information about Titus for three and a half years after he ran away. Where he went and how he acquired his military skills after he left the Corlies farm are 250-year-old mysteries.

Besides John Corlies searching for him in Shrewsbury, Titus faced other challenges. At six feet tall, he stood out when the average man's height was five-foot-nine. Not an enormous difference, but enough to attract second looks. To avoid apprehension on the road, he'd need a forged pass. Whoever wrote it for him (he was probably illiterate) knew his plans and might compromise him. His two slight advantages were passing as white (Titus was "not very black") and changing out of his slave garments (he escaped with "a quantity of clothes").

Titus may have pursued one or more of the following paths on his way to becoming Colonel Tye.

Would Titus Go Immediately to Sandy Hook?

Sandy Hook, tantalizingly close to mainland Shrewsbury and within easy reach of his Rumson home, was the initial waypoint for Titus. He knew the Navesink and Shrewsbury Rivers, their streams and coves and safe anchorages. Titus might have swum across the narrows of the Shrewsbury to get to the Hook or stolen a small boat to row there under the cover of darkness. The danger was that the lighthouse keeper at Sandy Hook, local fishermen or clammers would notice a stranger showing up and maybe even recognize him. In 1775, Sandy Hook was not a long-term safe haven for a runaway.

Quakers May Have Helped Titus Escape

Titus faced serious problems running away by himself, no matter where he headed. His closest allies were the Shrewsbury Quakers who had visited John Corlies. They might have sheltered Titus for several nights while he figured out his next destination. Titus could pretend that he was still enslaved when a Quaker took him to New York to sell produce. It's possible that sympathetic Quakers bought him passage on a ship.

Quakers could have given Titus the locations of safe houses, using an early version of what came to be called the Underground Railroad. George Washington once complained about "a slave escaping from Alexandria to Philadelphia, whom a society of Quakers, formed for such purposes attempted to liberate."

Did Titus Pretend to Be a Free Man in New York?

If he got to New York in late 1775, Titus might escape notice despite Corlies's newspaper ad. He'd be one of hundreds of other Black men, enslaved and free. Nonetheless, he'd face ten long months in hiding until the British occupied New York the following September. Maybe Titus spent only a few days in the city before stowing away or finding work on an outbound ship.

Did Titus Travel to Virginia?

The most repeated legend is that Titus was lured to Virginia by Dunmore's promise of freedom for slaves. It plays, however, like a retroactive supposition based on what is known about him later in the war.

The reasoning was that Dunmore had a regiment of Black soldiers and Titus became a military leader, ergo, he must have joined Dunmore's Ethiopian Regiment. As logical as this may seem, Titus would have faced formidable obstacles getting to Virginia.

Shrewsbury to Norfolk was a treacherous 360-mile trip for a runaway, made all the more difficult when Maryland began to guard its borders closest to Virginia. Going overland on poor and unconnected roads was impractical and time-consuming. Just to get through south Jersey, Titus would have to buy or steal horses or pay for or beg wagon rides. He'd have to hire a boat to cross the Delaware River at Cape May or Salem Counties.

Delaware was halfway to Norfolk. Still ahead for a furtive traveler was the long Delmarva Peninsula and another water crossing at Chesapeake Bay. A road trip like this would take weeks—possible but improbable.

The fastest and safest option was going by ship. With money, luck and favorable weather, Titus might make Norfolk by late November in 1775.

Did Titus Actually Join the Ethiopian Regiment?

As Samuel A. Forman noted, "Once in Virginia, Titus trained and saw combat as a British soldier, remaining undeterred even when his unit was decimated by a smallpox outbreak. Traveling back north to British-occupied New York City and now styling himself 'Colonel Tye,' he had become a competent and aggressive leader of Loyalist irregulars. He commanded soldiers of both races on daring raids targeting Patriots deep in Monmouth County."

As compelling as this story is, there's a major problem with it: there's no evidence. Titus is not on any of the Ethiopian Regiment rosters archived at the University of Virginia's Williamsburg Library. Yes, as John Corlies suggested, Titus could have used an alias, but once he was with Dunmore, he'd have little reason for an alter ego. His fame as "Tye" several years later suggests that he was proud of his name and unafraid to use it.

The majority of the runaways who fled to Dunmore were from Norfolk and Princess Anne Counties in Virginia. The governor was dubious that they could become effective fighters, returning some to their enslavers who promised to take loyalty oaths to the British Crown.

Dunmore made no concerted effort to turn these men into an effective fighting force. Most of their training consisted of learning to march in formation. It's doubtful that they were even issued standard British military uniforms. A few wore smocks embroidered with the slogan "Liberty to Slaves."

By and large, Dunmore used his Ethiopian troops for the kinds of physical labor they'd done while enslaved. Some dug defensive trenches around

Runaway slaves in Dunmore's Ethiopian Regiment. *Great Bridge (VA) Battlefield & Waterways History Foundation.*

Norfolk; others conducted foraging expeditions, stealing cattle and foodstuffs from remote countryside farms in Virginia.

The British rarely entrusted Black soldiers with guns. Dunmore said that he had "about 50 Negroes who I now arm and discipline as fast as they come in....I am now endeavoring to raise two Regiments, one of white people, called the Queen's Own Loyal Virginia Regiment, the other of Negroes called Lord Dunmore's Ethiopian Regiment." Although he gave them muskets for a battle at Great Bridge in December 1775, Dunmore provided no weaponry training.

All things considered, if Titus actually was in Virginia, he would have picked up little military expertise.

How and When Did Titus Return to New Jersey?

Accompanied by his staff and their families, Dunmore retreated to a one-hundred-ship flotilla in Chesapeake Bay. Very few Ethiopian troops were allowed in his so-called Floating Town. Most were stranded on shore. Dispirited, those left behind took advantage of a pardon offer and went back to their former owners.

The Ethiopians on the ships suffered under poor living conditions, made worse when typhus and smallpox broke out. In February 1776, Dunmore put them in "a pretty good barracks" north of Portsmouth. They were made to dig defensive trenches again.

Additional Virginia runaways increased the land-based Ethiopian Regiment to between two and three hundred. Facing continual rebel pressure, Dunmore moved his government ships again at the end of May. By then, disease had felled half the Ethiopians.

In August 1776, Governor Dunmore and "his ragamuffins" left Virginia in seven ships to rendezvous with General William Howe at Staten Island. If Titus had trained with Dunmore, he could have been one of the "Blacks and Tories number[ing] one hundred and twenty total" on board those ships. Or perhaps Titus was among the eight hundred Black regiment troops already on Staten Island. Either way, he'd be eager to let the British know about his firsthand knowledge of Sandy Hook and its environs. The British would realize that this unique intelligence source had both the passion and the ability to help them defeat the Monmouth County rebels.

Perhaps Titus Became a Black Pioneer

During a North Carolina expedition in the spring of 1776, British General Henry Clinton organized about seventy runaways from the Carolinas and Georgia into a company he called the Black Pioneers. He promised them emancipation at the end of the war. White officers commanded the Pioneers. They were not combat soldiers but support troops who dug ditches, cleared roads, cut trees and built fortifications and barracks, the kinds of work military engineers do today. The Pioneers were never a completely contiguous force. Companies of perhaps thirty or so Pioneers were assigned to assist larger white units.

After a brief assignment at Newport, Rhode Island, the Pioneers joined Sir William Howe's occupation of New York City in September 1776. If Titus was on Staten Island, he might have been assigned to the Pioneers.

When Howe took Philadelphia one year later, the Pioneers were sent "to attend the scavengers, assist in cleaning the streets & removing all nuisances being thrown into the streets."

When the British abandoned the city in June 1778, the Black Pioneers literally blazed a path for them on the long march across New Jersey. Despite these intriguing possibilities, no records indicate that Titus was a Pioneer during any these operations.

Was Titus a Queen's Ranger?

Did Titus get to Sandy Hook as part of a special fighting unit? In his reminiscences, British Lieutenant Colonel John Graves Simcoe wrote about the famous Queen's Rangers. Named to honor Queen Charlotte, they were formed on Staten Island from New York and New Jersey Loyalist recruits. The all-white Rangers were combined with Dunmore's Loyal Virginia Regiment when he arrived in August 1776.

Simcoe took command of the Rangers in Philadelphia in October 1777. The Rangers were supplemented with elements of the Black Brigade. Simcoe believed in the value of Black troops, having previously tried to create a Loyalist regiment of free Blacks in Boston. Later in the war, he took a harsher position, insisting that "able bodied men slaves…would have their liberty…provided they come without their wives and children." That restriction would not have mattered to Titus because as far as we know he never married.

A Black Pioneer. *Bob Graham.*

Five hundred Rangers were part of Colonel Charles Mawhood's expeditionary force at Salem, New Jersey, in March 1778. They marched inland, foraging for supplies along the way. The Rangers surprised and slaughtered "the insolent rebels" at Quinton's Bridge and three days later at Hancock's Bridge.

Colonel John Graves Simcoe. *Public domain.*

Advancing toward Monmouth Court House in June 1778, the Queen's Rangers ravaged the Jersey countryside, absconding with food, livestock and other necessary supplies. Simcoe recalled that "he had also many Refugees with him, who served as guides...the chief of his guides was born at Monmouth." Simcoe doesn't specify his chief guide's name or race. We have no evidence that man was Titus.

Titus in the Black Brigade

We know that Titus was operating from Sandy Hook by 1779, but he may have been there two years earlier. The British used local guides as lead elements during a skirmish in February 1777 when they attacked the Monmouth Militia on the Highlands hills. Titus, who was raised on the southern side of the Navesink River, would have been an ideal guide during the battle (see chapter 8). The British regularized these men into a semi-official military unit, the Black Brigade, at the end of 1777. Titus developed and demonstrated his leadership skills at Sandy Hook.

The Battle of Navesink was fought on the hills (*far right*) west of Sandy Hook. *Library of Congress.*

Some Black Brigade fighters brought their families with them when they joined the British on the Hook. Single runaway women such as the enslaved Sarah Jones were there too. Jones and her ten-year-old son, Isaac, fled the control of Richard Stout, the constable who compiled Middletown's 1771 slaveholder list.

CHAPTER 6

CORLIES IN THE REVOLUTION

The whole of his Letters were carried off,
& no person could give an account of them.
—John Hancock

John Corlies Jr., the enslaver and excommunicated Quaker, was also a Loyalist spy. In July 1776, a few days after the Declaration of Independence was issued, he was with Joseph Wardell and George Allen sailing to General William Howe's camp on Staten Island. The Shrewsbury men said that Colonel George Taylor of the Monmouth Militia gave them passes for crossing enemy lines to recover runaway slaves. If Corlies suspected that Titus was there, he didn't find him on Staten Island. Howe gave the three men some other runaways to take back with them as a consolation.

George Washington was well aware of the build-up on Staten Island:

> *Camp on Long-Island, July 21, 1776, two o'clock. To his Excellency General Washington, Head-Quarters, New-York.*
>
> *SIR: Colonel Hand reports seven large ships are coming up from the Hook to the narrows.*
>
> *A negro belonging to one Strickler, at Gravesend, was taken prisoner (as he says) last Sunday at Coney-Island. Yesterday he made his escape, and was taken prisoner by the rifle-guard. He reports eight hundred negroes collected on Staten-Island, this day to be formed into a regiment. I am your Excellency's most obedient humble servant, N*[athanael] *Green.*

Lord Howe's fleet anchored at the Narrows between Long Island and Staten Island. *New York Public Library.*

Left: Admiral Richard Howe. *Public domain.*

Right: General William Howe. *Public domain.*

The Turncoat Taylor

The trio's other mission was to feel out the reception Colonel Taylor would get if he switched sides. Taylor had just witnessed 138 ships, loaded with thirty-two thousand troops, arrive at Sandy Hook. One observer described the scene as "a wood of pine trees trimmed....I could not believe my eyes...the whole bay was as full of shipping as ever it could be, I declare that I thought all of London was afloat."

Commanded by William Howe's brother, Admiral Lord Richard Howe, the seemingly unstoppable force panicked Taylor. He realized that the British could easily defeat his small contingent of militiamen and very likely put down the entire rebellion for that matter. He was afraid to lose everyone and everything dear to him at his Middletown home. Encouraged by what Corlies and the other emissaries to Staten Island found out, Taylor defected in November. The British put Taylor in charge of Sandy Hook, a place very near his 220-acre farm.

The brick Sandy Hook Lighthouse was erected in 1764 to guide ships into New York Harbor. Its strategic location made its control a high priority for both sides during the war. Early in 1776, the New York Provincial Congress ordered Major William Malcolm to "use your best discretion to render the light-house entirely useless."

On March 6, Malcolm's rebel troops had done just that, removing the lighthouse lenses and lamps. Malcolm gave Colonel George Taylor some of the booty, including "eight copper lamps, two tackle falls and blocks, and three casks, and a part of a cask of oil from the dismantling of the beacon."

The British responded quickly. In May, they took control of the Hook for the duration of the war. When the turncoat George Taylor was given command of the lighthouse, he returned the stolen lamps and equipment.

John Corlies, British Spy

On the other side of New Jersey, one Saturday evening in October 1776, an American military courier was drinking in the Fountain Inn. The public house at Bristol, Pennsylvania, on the Delaware River was located alongside the ferry landing to Burlington, New Jersey. Early in the Revolutionary War, Patriot soldiers shot up the tavern's sign because it depicted King George

Sandy Hook Lighthouse. *Public domain.*

The Fountain Inn on the Delaware River. *Public domain.*

John Hancock. *National Park Service.*

III, the hated English monarch. They repainted it with an image of General George Washington.

Chatting with a stranger that fall evening, courier Timothy Dodd indiscreetly mentioned that he was transporting a packet of documents from George Washington. His eager listener, none other than John Corlies, deliberately got his new acquaintance inebriated. The drinks "made him fuddled…whereupon Dodd left…his Bundle in the Barr Room while he slept; on his return the whole of his Letters were carried off, & no person could give an account of them."

The episode caused American leaders plenty of anguish. John Hancock wrote to Washington, "As your Letters may be of utmost Consequence, & the Enemy may derive great Advantages from the Knowledge of their Contents, as I have no Doubt but they will soon be in possession of them." Hancock was prescient—the stolen letters did wind up with British General William Howe. News of Washington's plans could provide the British with a tactical advantage.

William Livingston, New Jersey's governor, was determined to punish the thief. "There is great reason to believe that a certain John Curlis [*sic*] of Shrewsbury in New Jersey was concerned in taking at Bristol the packet from General Washington to Congress." A Congressional Committee, acknowledging that Corlies would be hard to find, offered "a £500 Reward to apprehend the Person." Corlies was never caught.

As disastrous as it might have been, worry over the stolen letters was overwrought. In December 1776, Colonel John Cadwalader stayed at the Fountain Inn while his troops waited to cross the Delaware to assist General Washington at the Battle of Trenton. Due to ice in the river, Cadwalader wasn't able to cross with his artillery and wasn't part of the battle. Fortunately, Washington was able to win the battle without Cadwalader and his men. On a blustery Christmas night, Washington surprised and defeated Hessian soldiers stationed there by the British.

Chapter 7

JEWSTOWN/COLTS NECK

There is nothing which has been contrived by man,
by which so much happiness is produced, as by a good tavern.
—Samuel Johnson

Just a few houses straddled the road from Freehold to Shrewsbury. The tiny village called Jewstown was anchored by a tavern and a store owned by Levy Hart. The Jewish merchant was an anomaly in a community of Baptists, Puritans, Quakers, Church of Englanders and Dutch Reformed.

Levy and his cousin Jonas Solomon were most likely born in London, England. Their parents, Ashkenazi Jews, had emigrated from Prussia. Levy and Jonas left for New York in the middle of 1755. The two men, who may not have been religiously observant, survived by peddling household goods on the city's streets. They applied for naturalization and were required to wait seven years before becoming American citizens.

Jewish Life in Monmouth County

The *New York Mercury* and other newspapers were full of enticing offers. Lured by advertisements touting New Jersey's growing population and its need for British manufactured goods, Hart and Solomon began to sell their wares in Middlesex and Monmouth Counties. Early success led Solomon to

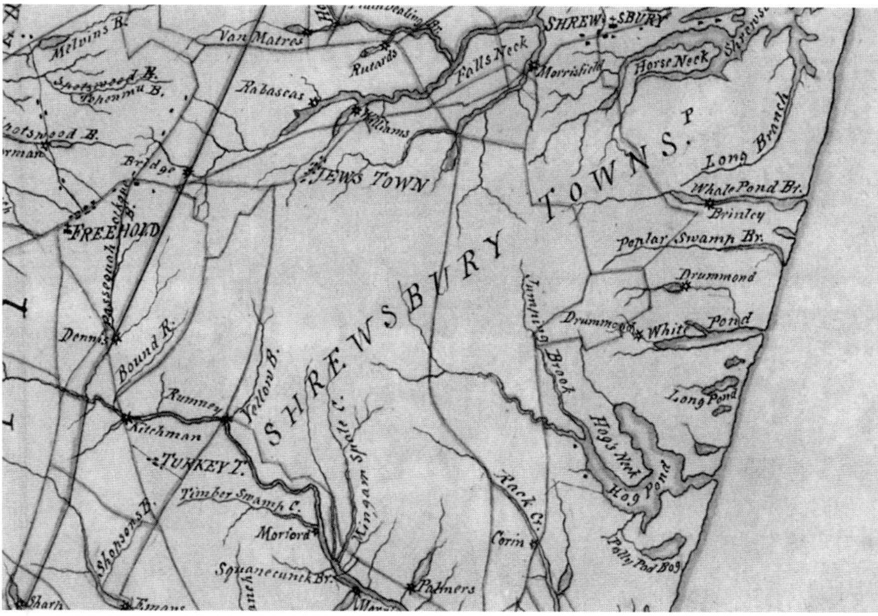

Jewstown (*center, top*) in 1769. *Library of Congress.*

purchase land in West Freehold for a farm. Both men settled permanently in Monmouth.

Selling door to door one afternoon, Levy Hart walked up the dirt road to Jacob Applegate's home in Middletown. The farmer, his wife and two grown daughters were Christians. In their late twenties, Catherine and Hannah Applegate were considered spinsters beyond marrying age.

Levy was soon a regular visitor at the Applegates' home. They were eager for his wares—he was interested in a wife. Despite differences in their religions, Jacob began to see Levy as a prospective suitor. When Levy introduced Jonas Solomon to the retired farmer, Jacob thought that he'd doubled his luck.

Jacob Applegate figured that the property-owning Solomon would be a good provider. He gave Jonas permission to marry Hannah in December 1757. Jacob was a bit more cautious with Hart, who was, after all, an itinerant peddler. He had Levy sign a £500 marriage bond, guaranteed by Applegate's friend Cornelius Vanderveer. Within days of his cousin's wedding, Levy Hart married Catherine Applegate.

Catherine and Levy Hart had three children by 1762, the year they bought fifty acres "by Hockhockson Brook where it flows into Wintapeck Bogg, by

Names of the Persons Naturalized.	Their Religious Profession.	Their Temporall Profession and Place of Abode.	Minister Certifying Receiving the Sacrament.	The Names of the Witnesses to the Certificate.	The Month & Year.
Isaac Nunes Henriques	Jew.	......	......	......	Oct. 28, 1741.
Abraham De Leas...........	Do.	......	......	......	......
Moses Levy..................	Jew.	of the City of New York. Merchant.	.....	......	Aprill 19, 1743.
Isaac Seixas................	Jew.	of the City of New York. Merchant.	......	......	Novr 4, 1745
Jacob Rodrigues Rivera.....	Jew.	of the Same City. Merchant.	......	......	Jan. 21, 1746.
Isaac Hays..................	Jew.	of the Same City. Tallow Chandler.	......	......	April 26, 1748.
Moses Benjamin Franks.....	Jew.	of the Same City.	......	......	Octr 18, 1748.
Isaac Adolphus..............	Jew.	Do. Trader.	......	... .	July 27, 1758.
Hyam Myers................	Jew.	Do. Butcher.	......	......	Jan'y 16, 1759.
Manuel Myers...............	Do.	Do. Trader.	......	......	Jan'y 16, 1759.
Isaac Elizer	Jew.	Rhode Island. Merchant.	......	......	July 23, 1763.
Levy Hart..................	Jew.	Colony of New York. Merchant.	......	....	Octobr 27, 1763.
Jonas Solomons............	Do.	Do. Do.	......	......	Octobr 27, 1763.
Napthaly Hart Meyers.......	Jew.	City of New York. Merchant.	......	......	April 27, 1764.
Joseph Jesurum Pinto	Jew.	Do. Minister of Jewish Congn.	......	......	Jan'y 22d 1766.

The 1763 naturalization records of Levy Hart and Jonas Solomon. *Jewish Heritage Museum of Monmouth County.*

a highway leading to a bridge over Mine Brook on the road from Freehold to Shrewsbury." Jacob Applegate lent the couple £318 for the purchase, with the proviso that Catherine's name appear on the deed. This unusual arrangement ensured that she would keep control of the property if the marriage didn't work out.

The Harts would operate a tavern on their property. Jonas Solomon did the same in Freehold. There was no question about their right to own legitimate businesses. The cousins became naturalized American citizens in 1763.

The Hart Inn and Tavern on the Old Burlington Path was conveniently located for travelers on the three-day stagecoach trip between Philadelphia and the seashore. The clear brook stream meandering by their back door provided an ample supply of fresh water. As their family grew, the Harts added a two-story home next to the tavern.

Hart and Solomon partnered to get better prices for business necessities but ran into problems nonetheless.

Freehold Court records show that the pair were part of dozens of Common Pleas filings. As defendants, they were accused of nonpayment of "Diverse Goods, Wares & Merchandises." Sometimes they filed suits to recover money from customers and debtors.

Levy and Catherine Hart were more prosperous than Jonas and Hannah Solomon. Jonas begged his father-in-law for a loan in 1765. Disappointed that he had misjudged his son-in-law's business acumen, Jacob Applegate nonetheless gave him a £120 mortgage but insisted once again that the deed be put in his daughter's name.

Jacob Applegate died in 1768, still not convinced that Jonas Solomon could take care of Hannah and their five children. Jacob bequeathed Hannah part of his farm land. Her sister, Catherine, more well off, got three cows and sixty pounds. As grateful as they were for these inheritances, the Solomons

The Hart Inn and Tavern would have looked like this around 1770. *Public domain.*

and Harts were just as thankful for another kind of property Jacob left them: two human beings.

The 1771 list of Shrewsbury slaveholders shows that Levy Hart and Jonas (John) Solomon each owned one person, genders not listed. These slaves surely worked in their owners' taverns, did domestic home chores and performed farm labor.

When Levy Hart died a few years later, his property inventory included just one slave, named Rose. When Catherine died in 1787, she owned an unidentified "Negro Girl" born around 1774 who could have been Rose's daughter. We know of no male slaves owned by the Harts. This leaves the intriguing possibility that the girl's father was either Levy Hart (fifty-four years old) or his son Jacob (fifteen). The three other Hart boys were younger than thirteen.

Jonas Solomon, overwhelmed with a crushing £1,000 debt and facing incarceration, abandoned Hannah, leaving her and their six children. He fled to North Carolina, where he changed his name to avoid responsibility for his business and personal failures in New Jersey.

The bereft Hannah Solomon was fortunate when her eldest daughter, Catherine, married Moses Mount Jr. in 1774. The couple took over her father's business, renaming it Mount's Tavern. The Solomon home and

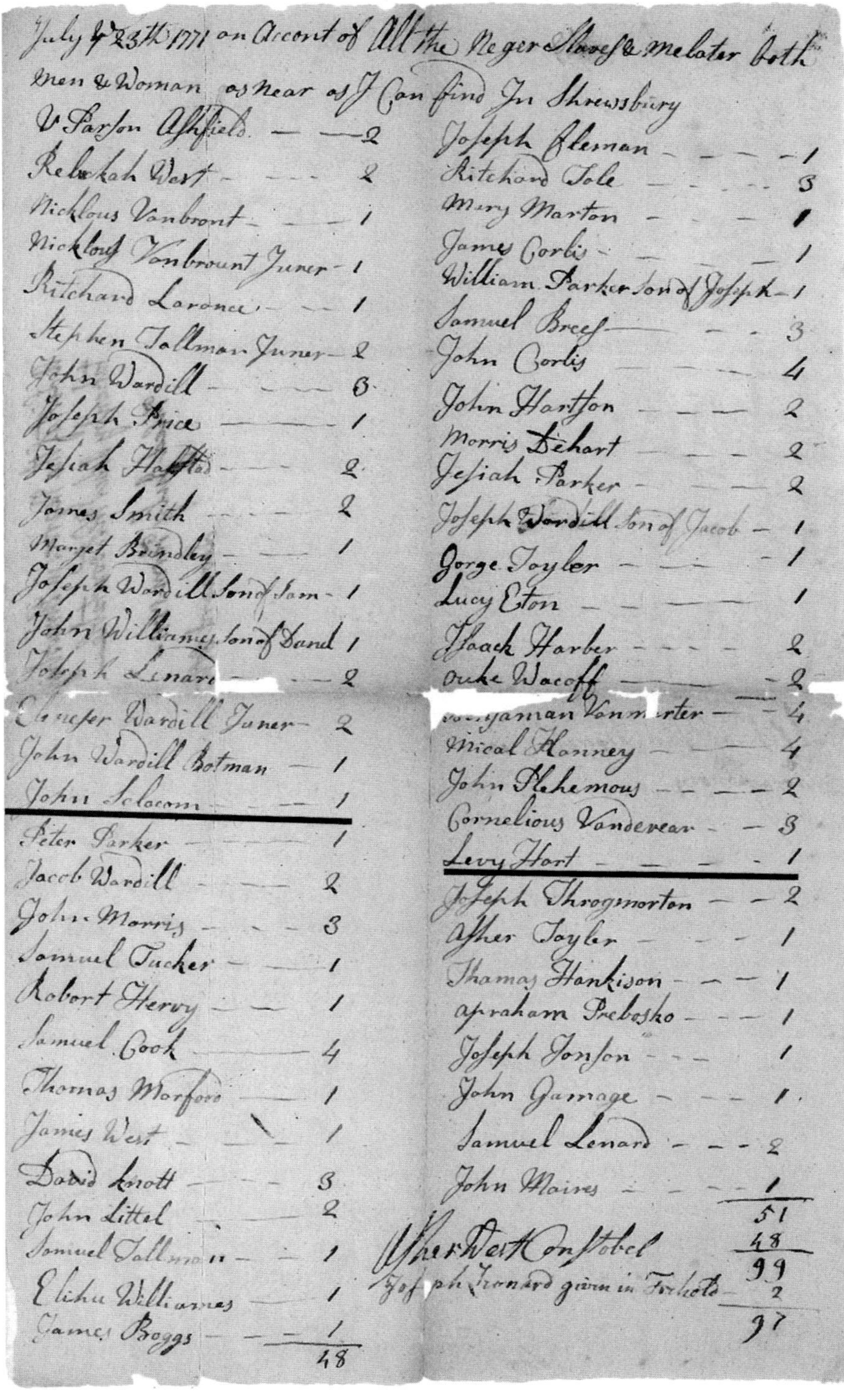

July ye 23th 1771 on Accont of All the Neger Slaves & melater both men & Woman as near as I Can find In Shrewsbury

Parson Ashfield	2
Rebekah West	2
Nicklous Vanbront	1
Nicklous Vanbrount Juner	1
Ritchard Laronce	1
Stephen Tallman Juner	2
John Wardill	3
Joseph Price	1
Josiah Halsted	2
James Smith	2
Marget Brindley	1
Joseph Wardill Son of Sam	1
John Williames Son of Danl	1
Joseph Lenard	2
Ebenezer Wardill Juner	2
John Wardill Botman	1
John Solacom	1
Peter Parker	1
Jacob Wardill	2
John Morris	3
Samuel Tucker	1
Robert Hervy	1
Samuel Cook	4
Thomas Morford	1
James West	1
David Knott	3
John Littel	2
Samuel Tallman	1
Elihu Williames	1
James Boggs	1
	48

Joseph Fleman	1
Ritchard Tole	3
Mery Marton	1
James Corlis	1
William Parker Son of Joseph	1
Samuel Brees	3
John Corlis	4
John Hartson	2
Morris Dehart	2
Josiah Parker	2
Joseph Wardill Son of Jacob	1
Jorge Tayler	1
Lucy Eton	1
Isaack Harber	2
Ouke Wacoff	2
Benjaman Vanmarter	4
Mical Hanney	4
John Plahemous	2
Cornelious Vandevear	3
Levy Hart	1
Joseph Throgmorton	2
Asher Tayler	1
Thomas Hankison	1
Aproham Prebosko	1
Joseph Jonson	1
John Gamage	1
Samuel Lenard	2
John Maires	1
	51
Usher West Constobel	48
	99
Joseph Lenard given in Frehold	2
	97

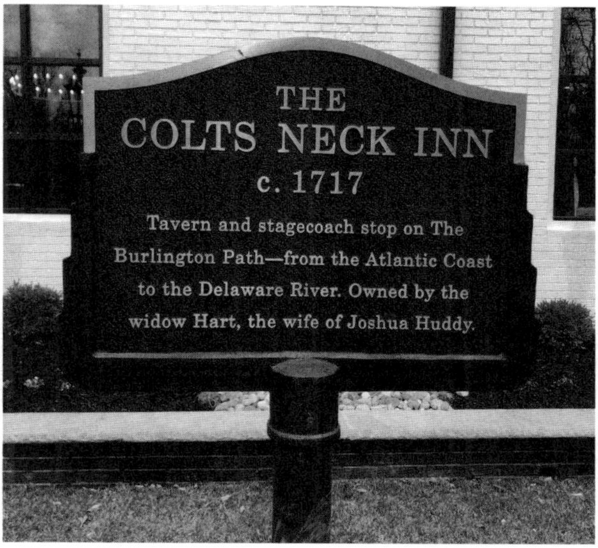

Opposite: Hart and Solomon on the 1771 Shrewsbury enslavers list. *Monmouth County Archives.*

Right: Sign at today's Colts Neck Inn. *Rick Geffken.*

business at Mount's Corner would bear witness to the dramatic events about to impact Freehold.

Hannah's sister, Catherine, would soon suffer her own marriage misfortune. Levy Hart died in September 1775, a few months after he obtained his last tavern license. The widow tried to maintain Hart's Tavern with the help of her two eldest children, Rebecca and Jacob (named for his grandfather but called by his middle name, John). They scraped by, doing everything they could for themselves and the five younger Hart children.

Revolutionary Turmoil

The family situation became more precarious when the colonial rebellion against British rule spilled over into armed conflict. Because rebel fighters frequented Hart's, the tavern became a refuge and a target. A careful businesswoman would keep her feelings about the war private, but Catherine probably favored the cause of independence. Her brothers Sylvester and Ebenezer were in the militia. One particular militiaman would soon come to dominate Catherine's life.

Chapter 8

HUDDY AT THE CROSSROADS

In this apparently happy and thriving province the approaching war was to work such havoc and cause such internal convulsions as were scarcely paralleled in any other part of America…life became feverish and uncertain.
—Leonard Lundin

New Jersey is called the "Crossroads of the Revolution" because more Revolutionary battles were fought in the state than in any other. American General Nathanael Greene wrote about "ravages in the Jerseys [that] exceed all description. Men slaughtered, women ravaged, and houses plundered, little girls not yet ten-years-old ravished, mothers and daughters ravaged in [the] presence of the husband and sons obliged to be spectators to their brutal conduct." Joshua Huddy became famous in defending Monmouth County, which suffered the worst of the bloodshed.

Huddy Gone Missing

Joshua Huddy disappeared from Salem in 1773 to avoid certain arrest and possible reimprisonment. Titus ran away from Shrewsbury two years later to escape the prison of slavery. Both men were out of sight for years until huge and consequential events beyond their control propelled them to prominence—and ultimately into head-to-head combat.

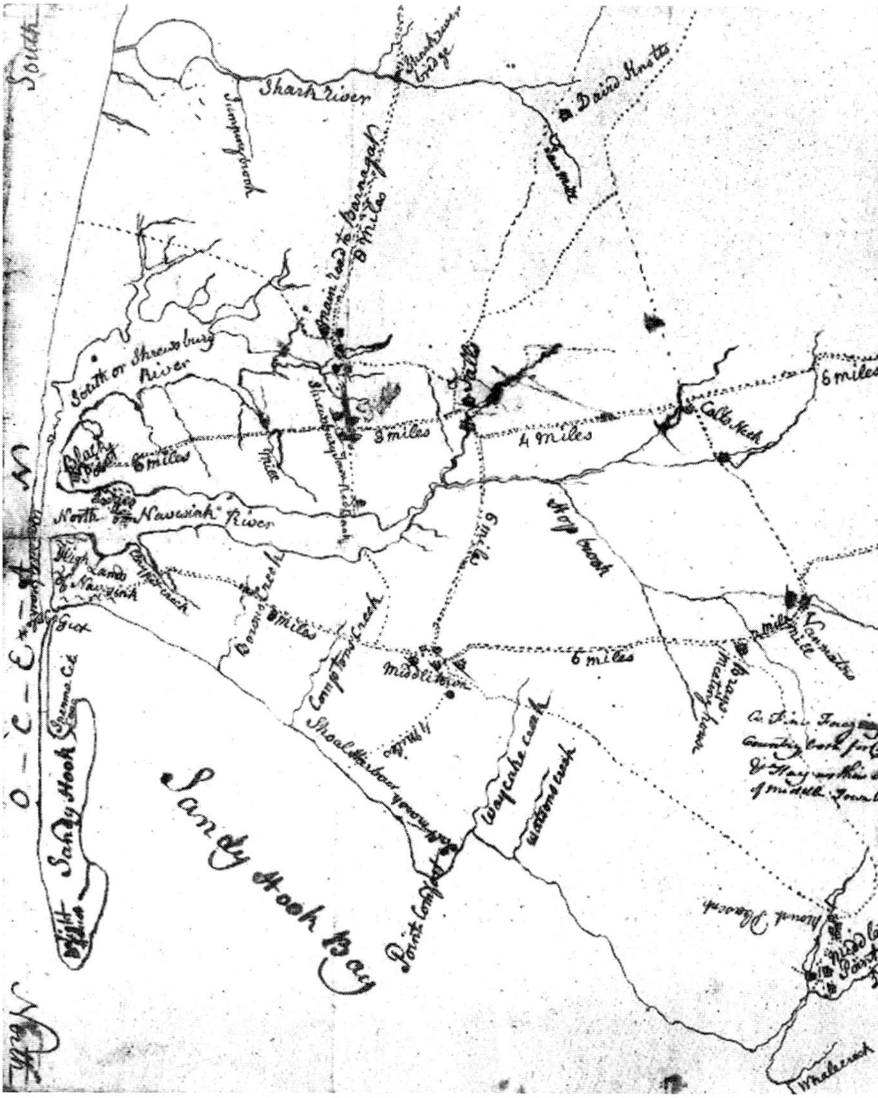

Colonel Elisha Lawrence's map of foraging sites. *Monmouth County Historical Association.*

No one knows Joshua Huddy's whereabouts for three years after he left Salem. Was he living with one of his siblings? Did he live under an assumed name? Did he move in with relatives in Burlington? Did he try farming again or piloting boats between the ports of Philadelphia? Most intriguingly, could he have joined a Pennsylvania militia troop?

Huddy's reemergence happened after two minor but significant military clashes Monmouth County. There's no evidence that he took part in either, but his subsequent rise to fame may be connected to them nonetheless.

In December 1776, Colonel Elisha Lawrence, a former Monmouth County sheriff from Upper Freehold, recruited Loyalists to fight against their rebellious neighbors. He sketched a crude map of the best places to loot cattle, supplies and foodstuffs from remote farms vulnerable to raids.

A regiment of Pennsylvania Continentals under Colonel Francis Gurney confronted Lawrence's inexperienced troops near Freehold on January 2. After a short exchange of intense fire, the Loyalists retreated. Some went to British-controlled Sandy Hook. They were henceforth called Refugees because they'd been forced to leave their homes and livelihoods.

For the next five years, these embittered Loyalists, white and Black, conducted inland forays. One chronicler reported that they "usually spared nothing. All things portable were borne along with them, farms were swept clean of stock, what could not be taken was destroyed, and homes were left in ashes."

The Battle of Navesink

Colonial militias were originally created in the seventeenth century to defend their towns and municipalities during emergencies. Revolutionary militiamen were local farmers and businessmen called up to serve for limited periods. Their civilian occupations were vital during the war as well, and these men were usually anxious to resume those roles and return to their families and farms. Their mixed motives for serving included obligation, patriotism, profits or even revenge. These part-time civilian soldiers were not a well-trained military force, especially in the early years of the war.

In February 1777, Monmouth militiamen were stationed at Highlands monitoring British ship movements in and around Sandy Hook Bay. Colonel Nathaniel Scudder's 140 undertrained men were camped in the hills around Esek Hartshorne's home. On the south side of the Navesink River at Black Point (probably at his brother John's house), another militia group had secured a British provision ship wrecked on a coastal beach.

Reports of this activity prompted the British Twenty-Sixth Regiment of Foot and some New Levies (volunteers) to sail from Staten Island on the twenty-eight-gun HMS *Syren*. They picked up Refugee guides at Sandy

Livingston's Sugar House on Liberty Street in New York. *Public domain.*

Hook before splitting into two groups. One detachment landed on the coast, scared off the militia and reclaimed what was left on the stranded provision ship.

The *Syren* brought a larger expeditionary force through an inlet into the Navesink River. They clambered onto ship's boats and landed at Rocky Point, out of sight of the hilltop militia. Black guides (Titus may have been one) led them through the snow-covered hills on a miserable winter's night.

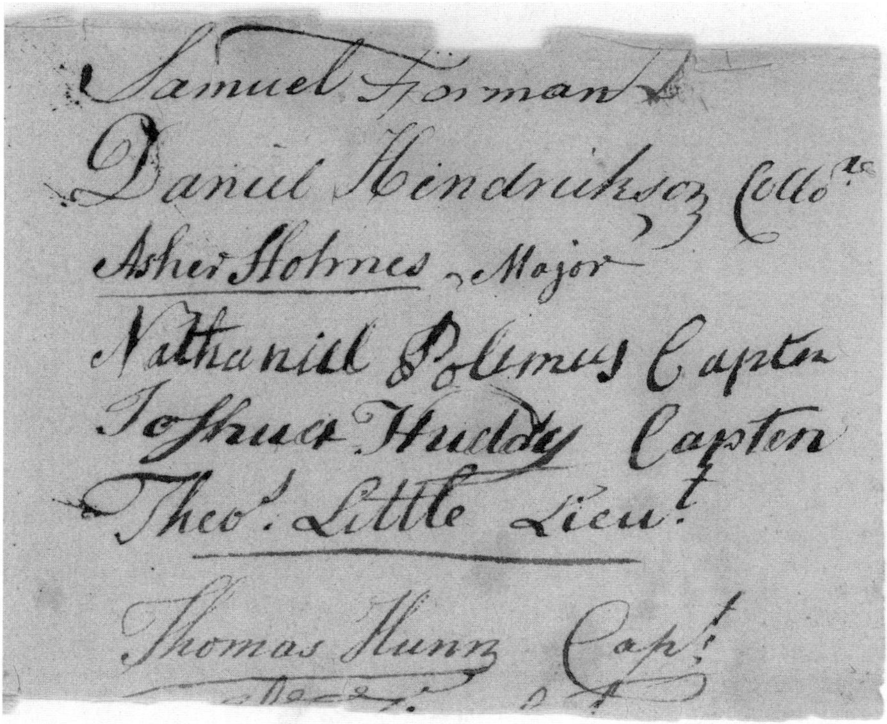

Samuel Forman
Daniel Hendrickson Collo
Asher Holmes Major
Nathaniell Polhemus Capten
Joshua Huddy Capten
Theo. Little Lieut.
Thomas Hunn Capt.

Above: Joshua Huddy's signature on a 1777 petition. *Monmouth County Historical Association.*

Left: Colonel David Forman. *Monmouth County Historical Association.*

The unsuspecting militia was quickly overwhelmed; at least four were killed (an early report said twenty-five) and seventy-two captured. Forty or so men escaped into the woods, some dying of their wounds. Joshua Huddy was not on Colonel David Forman's list of the Navesink prisoners of war. Was Huddy one of the men who escaped capture?

The February 13 battle at Navesink was a brief skirmish that turned into a rout. The American prisoners were taken to the horrid Livingston's Sugar House prison in New York. It was one of several storage facilities originally built to refine sugar and molasses imported from the Caribbean. So many perished in these jails from malnutrition and disease (estimates up to eighteen thousand) that a survivor noted that "the prisoners were dying daily like rotten sheep."

A century later, Livingston's was still remembered as

> *one of the chief dens of human torture…its sweetness to be changed to gall and bitterness, and its cheerful business hum to the sighs and wails of the suffering and starving….Within these wall were at times huddled 400 or 500 prisoners of war, without beds, blankets, or fire in winter, wearing for months the filthy garments that covered them on the day of their capture. Hot weather came, and with it the typhus fever, which prevailed fearfully, filling the dead cart on each returning morning with wrecks of wasted humanity, which were rudely dumped in the trenches on the outskirts of the city. The meagre diet of these suffering patriots consisted of pork and sea biscuit; the latter having been damaged by salt water, were consequently very mouldy, and much worm-eaten.*

Huddy's Rise

Captain Joshua Huddy joined thirty-four other Monmouth Militia officers in May petitioning New Jersey's government to establish compulsory militia service. At the time, Huddy was in charge of an artillery company at Tinton Falls protecting Colonel Daniel Hendrickson's mill, which was being used as a magazine for powder, arms and military stores for the American army. Huddy and his men may also have attempted to restart the century-old ironworks to make cannonballs.

But how did this formerly incarcerated and wanted Salem County man become a Monmouth County militia officer in the spring of 1777? He had a powerful friend in David Forman, the American commander most responsible for Joshua Huddy's ascendency during the war.

Between 1776 and 1783, Forman simultaneously held the ranks of colonel of the Continental Army and general of the New Jersey State Troops. He was called George Washington's "sentinel on the Monmouth Coast" for his invaluable reports on British ship movements around Sandy Hook.

Forman was described by a supporter as "one of those fussy men sometimes met with, brave and faithful enough as a soldier, but half tyrant and half pomposity." Tories called him "Black David" because his harsh treatment of others revealed a "dark and devious soul." He was an enslaver, outraged when the British encouraged slaves to leave local farms and plantations.

Huddy's company, according to a military historian, was "equipped with three light field guns, and also…carried muskets…the command served as a field battery, with guns of position as garrison artillery, or as infantry." It was a versatile unit.

During Huddy's five months at Tinton Falls, he was not a commander to fool with. He personally pursued one of his artillery men who overstayed his leave in Freehold. An enraged Huddy rode to John Reed's home and took the man back to his duty station.

The lack of complete and contiguous military records for Joshua Huddy is partially explained by the part-time nature of militia service. He probably

The 1777 Battle of Germantown, Pennsylvania. *Public domain.*

American artillery men during the Revolution. *New York Public Library.*

served for six months at a time and then went back to his civilian occupations until the next call-up.

Nonetheless, Joshua Huddy stood up to every challenge, commanded his men with authority and was widely acknowledged by superior officers, political leaders and civilians as among the very best rebel combatants. He was unimpeachably brave and daring, exactly the kind of ruthless partisan you'd want on your side during a war.

From his first days with the militia, Huddy showed little regard or mercy for anyone he deemed a Loyalist. Former friends or neighbors he captured were summarily executed. He gained renown as the sworn enemy of "miscreants and desperadoes"—the Refugees who would seek revenge for his particular ruthlessness.

When George Washington's Continental Army battled William Howe's British army at Germantown, Pennsylvania, in October 1777, Joshua Huddy was there. His artillerymen were attached to Major Asher Holmes's First Regiment of the Monmouth Militia. Holmes described the scene in a letter to his wife:

> *Gen. Green*[e]*'s 'Listed Men to the right of us…all gave way except the Monmouth Militia and Gen. Forman's Red Coats* [they were wearing captured uniforms] *who stood firm and advanced upon the British Red Coats, who were at least three times our number, to a fence, where we made a stand. The fire was very severe, and the enemy ran. They brought a fieldpiece to fire on us with grapeshot, but our Monmouth men stood firm until their ammunition was nearly exhausted, and the enemy advancing around our right flank.…Providence seems to have protected our Monmouth Militia in a particular manner, as we have lost very few, if any, killed, and not many wounded.*

Although Howe defeated Washington at Germantown, the French foreign minister was impressed by the Continental Army's ability to stand up to British professional soldiers. Charles Gravier, comte de Vergennes, urged his government to support the emerging new nation, assistance that was key to the ultimate American victory. Vergennes played an extraordinary role in the story of Joshua Huddy (see chapter 16).

Legal Troubles

Legal infractions stalked Joshua Huddy as much as British Loyalists did. His rough-and-ready ways were an asset for fighting the British, but he was incapable of civil behavior. He pleaded guilty in January 1778 to a charge of assaulting Charles Gilmore of Middletown, possibly another of his militiamen. The quick-tempered Huddy paid a ten-dollar fine for "fisticuffs."

Later that year, Joshua Huddy intercepted a Shrewsbury woman named Elizabeth Pritchard trying to hide the belongings of her friend James Price, who had joined the British. Huddy believed that he had the right to the full value of the confiscated goods under a New Jersey law concerning seized illegal property. He felt entitled to the spoils of war.

Huddy sued Pritchard for what she was smuggling:

> *Eliz. Pritchard on 8 Oct 1778 at Shrewsbury...did attempt to convey from within the lines or some place in the possession of the subjects or troops of the King of Great Britain, certain goods, wares and merchandise of the value of £1,980, 7 shillings, and 11 pence, which said goods, wares, and merchandise...* [which were] *said to be brought from within the Lines of the Enemy.*

No records have been found showing that Huddy ever collected.

Second Marriage

Another of Huddy's men was an artillery matross from Freehold, Daniel Applegate. His duty was to stand side by side with the gunners, loading, firing and sponging the cannons.

Private Applegate may have introduced his cousin Catherine Hart to Joshua Huddy when they dropped by her tavern for a drink and a meal. The forty-three-year-old Hart, widowed for two years, was an attractive prospect, although any suitors might hesitate knowing that they'd have to provide for her seven minor children. That inconvenience did not deter the ambitious Joshua Huddy.

Three years her junior, he was intrigued as much by her property as by her potential as a wife. When the heat from Loyalist pursuers got too intense, Huddy had retreated to a hemlock grove just upstream from Hart's Tavern. The naturally formed cave along the clay bank of the Mine Brook was fine

Huddy and Hart's marriage record from the Dutch Reformed Church of Freehold and Middletown. *Monmouth County Historical Association.*

for temporary shelter, but Huddy saw Catherine's inn as the perfect place to plan his raids against the British—and, not incidentally, to enrich himself.

Dominie Benjamin DuBois. *Monmouth County Historical Association.*

Huddy charmed his way into another vulnerable woman's life, although their actual affections for each other are unknown. Catherine must have been naive to Huddy's real motives. She settled for a courtship of short visits, extended absences and ultimately plenty of worry.

Despite his military activities and distracting court cases, Huddy found time to marry Catherine on October 28, 1778. Dominie Benjamin DuBois conducted the ceremony. Remarkably, the former Quaker married the Protestant widow of a Jew at a Dutch Reformed Church.

Benjamin DuBois and Joshua Huddy, both from Salem County, had the same fierce temperament. While ministering at the Dutch Reformed Church of Freehold and Middletown, DuBois "frequently preached to his people on the subject of the war, exhorting them to do their duty faithfully to their country, and invariably he made their struggle for liberty the subject of his public prayers."

The fiery DuBois took an active role in raids against the British with the Monmouth Militia, earning him the sobriquet "the Fighting Parson." One Tory opponent remarked that he was "like a pack horse" patrolling with his gun and knapsack looking for Refugees.

Legal Troubles without End

If she expected security and supportive companionship in her new marriage, Catherine would be quickly disappointed. Joshua moved into her home and took control of her tavern business and considerable farm property. Never interested in domestic matters, Huddy brought discord into her family. He was often away with the militia, obsessed with fighting the British as well as his own best interests, not in the well-being of his

Above: Catherine and Joshua Huddy's Colts Neck house. *Public domain.*

Left: The only physical remnant of the Huddy house is this six-inch-long brass key. *Monmouth County Historical Association.*

wife's children. Raised by a kind and loving father, Levy Hart's offspring were unprepared for this nonconformist, rough-edged stepfather. They recognized Huddy's egotism and irascibility before their mother did, creating tensions within the household.

Huddy, believing that his marriage made him owner of all the Hart property, saw an opportunity to turn a quick buck. He and Catherine argued when she refused to allow the sale of her house, tavern and land. She pointed out that her son Jacob was a co-owner on the deed. The obstinate Huddy threatened to throw the entire family out.

The Monmouth County sheriff, Nicholas Van Brunt, intervened. He knew Huddy from their days together in the militia at Tinton Falls. Van Brunt persuaded Huddy to sign a bond for £15,000 as a guarantee against selling the family home and evicting the Hart children. If household peace was restored, it was a temporary truce at best.

Van Brunt filed suit in August 1779 to collect the bond, alleging that Huddy "did dispose of…certain goods and chattels formerly the property of the said Catherine his wife…without her consent and…by means of threats or blows prevented as well Rebecca [Hart] Longstreet, Jacob Hart & Ebenezer Hart, children of the said Catherine, from living & continuing with him & Catherine." The perpetually broke Huddy refused to pay.

Less than a year into the disastrous marriage, Catherine left Colts Neck. She and her children moved temporarily to the Freehold farm of her son-in law Elias's father, the widower John Longstreet.

How would Huddy work the farm he took over by himself? He had militia commitments and multiple legal difficulties. He lived with the constant fear of being captured—he knew that Joseph Murray had been killed while plowing his fields in Middletown. Huddy would be loath to plant, plow and harvest. His 1779 tax records show that he had one slave, probably the one Catherine brought into their marriage. Catherine may have taken the slave with her when she left, forcing Huddy to hire help, another drain on his meager financial resources.

Chapter 9
MONMOUTH COURT HOUSE

Washington's Continentals then stood toe-to-toe with the British, bloodily repulsing a series of powerful attacks by crack troops.
—Brendan Morrissey

Two years after the North American colonies declared independence from Great Britain, the longest single-day battle of the Revolutionary War took place in Monmouth County. On a blistering hot June day, a scofflaw turned Patriot and a runaway turned Refugee fought on opposite sides in the fields and hills around Old Tennent Church.

This episode in their intense rivalry makes for a compelling narrative—if only it had happened. Speculations that the two were at Monmouth Court House are assumptions based on the faulty memories of veterans, old men who mixed up wartime events. In fact, Joshua Huddy and Colonel Tye played peripheral roles after the battle.

The Trek

During most of the war, the British enjoyed a strategic advantage—their enormous fleet could move thousands of troops anywhere by water and did so largely unopposed. They did not have that option in 1778 in Philadelphia.

Left: General Sir Henry Clinton. *Public domain.*

Below: The British wagon train stretched for miles across New Jersey. *Public domain.*

Opposite: British soldiers ransacked many homes on their march. *Public domain.*

General Sir Henry Clinton correctly assessed the danger of the French fleet blockading the lower Delaware River and sailing up to bombard the city. The British navy would be incapable of rescuing his troops. Clinton was ordered to abandon Philadelphia and march across New Jersey, with New York the army's eventual destination.

The ninety-mile traverse from Pennsylvania to Sandy Hook was a ponderous slog. Clinton's long and slow wagon train was vulnerable to Washington's army. His wagons were overloaded because the "rich British officers had taken with them coaches, draught and saddle-horses in abundance; mistresses and their effects"—everything they owned and plundered during their occupation.

No one knew precisely when or by which routes the British would travel through Monmouth. Joshua Huddy's militia contingent spent days reconnoitering areas east of the village of Monmouth Court House.

DESTRUCTION AT FREEHOLD

The British destroyed virtually everything along their way, burning houses and taking food, horses and whatever else they coveted. The *New Jersey Gazette* reported, "The devastation they have made in some parts of Freehold exceeds perhaps any they have made…having in the Court-house burnt and destroyed eight dwelling houses, all on farms adjoining each other, besides barns and out-houses."

Hannah Solomon's West Freehold farm was one of those torched. She and her children frantically doused the threatening fires, barely saving their home. Thirteen-year-old Rebekah recalled watching the next day's battle from her rooftop. Her cousin Rebecca Hart, Catherine's daughter, watched it from horseback atop a nearby hill. The Solomon family survived the war, living on the rescued property for years afterward.

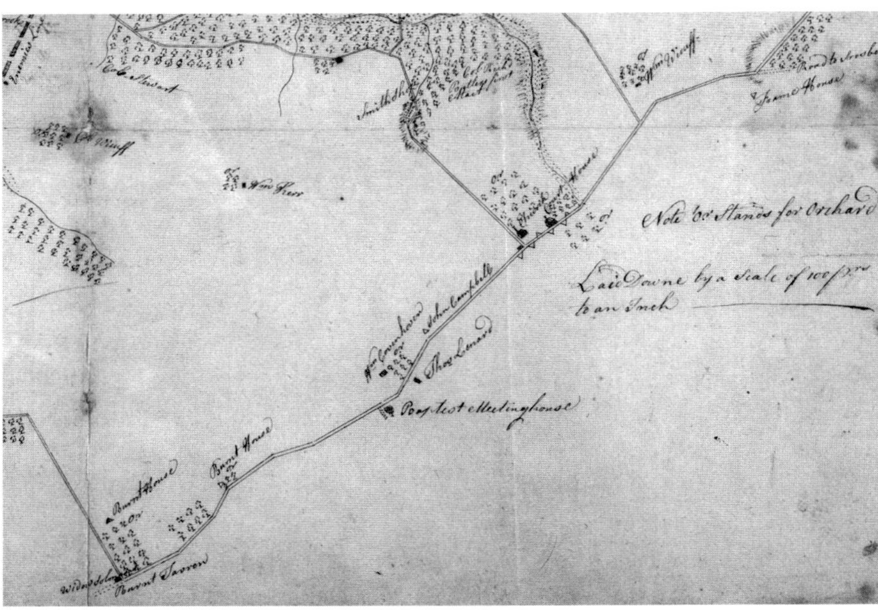

Above: A map of the British route to Freehold showing *(from lower left to upper right)* Widow Solomon, Burnt Tavern, another Burnt House and then William Covenhoven's home. *New York Historical Society.*

Opposite, top: The Covenhoven House on the Burlington Path. *Monmouth County Historical Association.*

Opposite, bottom: The first Monmouth Court House was located southwest of Freehold until 1731, when it was replaced by one on Main Street in town. *Public domain.*

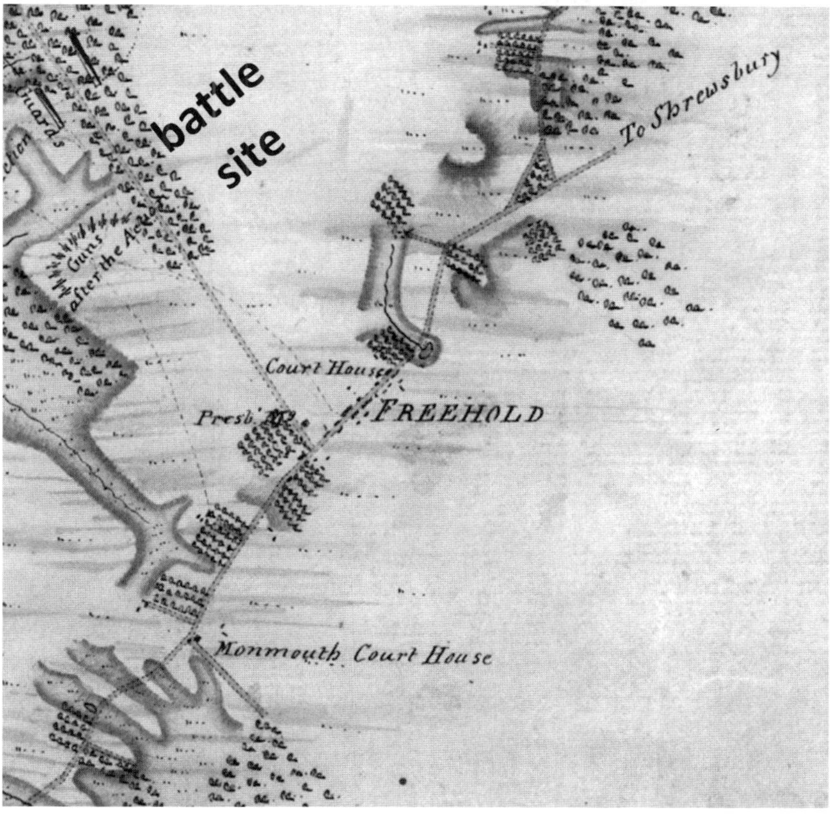
battle
site
To Shrewsbury
Court House
Presb.
FREEHOLD
Monmouth Court House

Battle of Monmouth by Emanuel Leutze. *Monmouth County Historical Association.*

Just up the road, William Covenhoven fled with as much of his furniture and household goods as he could manage. His wife, Elizabeth, refused to leave. When General Clinton commandeered the house for his headquarters on June 26, the seventy-three-year-old woman was forced to sleep on the floor of the milk room with her slaves and servants. She defiantly refused to buckle to British indignities, finally securing Clinton's promise to leave her home intact. Nonetheless, during the next two days, Clinton's soldiers took her clothing, cows and horses. When she begged Clinton to leave her Bible and a few books, he remarked, "Here you damned old rebel bitch, with one foot in the grave, take them." Clinton's troops left the Covenhoven home on the old Burlington Path without burning it down. The 275-year-old house survives to this day.

June 28, 1778, was a simmering, windless summer day when Washington's troops caught up with Clinton's army. A Massachusetts sergeant wrote, "This place is called Monmouth. It has been very hot all day. Numbers of our men had fainted and given out with the heat before we came up to the enemy."

American Colonel Israel Shreve recalled the brutality of that June day in a letter to his wife, Mary:

> *I have the pleasure to Inform you that yesterday a Battle was fought between His Excellency Gen. Washington and Gen. Clinton with part of their army. the Glory of the Day was Doubtful for five or six hours but at Last turned in the favour of us. the Enemy was Drove off the Ground. after it was over I viewed the field of Battle where many British Granedier and Light Infantry Lay Weltring in their Gore, among them Col: Monkton Col: Hide and many other Officers and three or four Hundred men, Last night they Retreated off* [and] *Left behind at Monmouth Courthouse fifty wounded among them several officers. we took near one hundred prisoners, our whole Loss is Inconsiderable, Colo: Bonner is killed with three other field officers, upon the whole it is Glorious for America, men was never more obstinate than the British yesterday, But forced to Give way to Americans, the Cannonade was heavier than Ever known on the field in America before, Colo: Barber of our Brigade Wounded through his side But I hope not mortal.*

David Forman's Continentals

The Monmouth Militia was not on the field at Monmouth. Perhaps some assumed that Joshua Huddy was there because of his close association with David Forman, who did take part in the battle. Historian John Rees relates:

> *Colonel David Forman's Additional Continental Regiment was formed in the spring of 1777, filled largely of men from Monmouth County, New Jersey. Despite being a home-grown organization, Forman was never able to enlist more than a hundred men, far below the number needed to form a complete regiment. By early July 1778, just thirty-eight days after the 28 June Battle of Monmouth, Forman's Regiment consisted of only four companies, numbering only seventy-four enlisted men; in 1778 a full regimental complement was 553 enlisted men.*

Nightfall brought an end to most of the fighting. Washington expected the battle to resume the next morning, but the British had other ideas. A Continental Army surgeon observed, "About 12 at Night the enemy marched off from the Court House in great haste leaving behind 4 wounded officers & 40 privates & a Surgn. to our mercy & fled to their shipping at Sandy Hook. Our officers and men (in general) behaved in the action with great

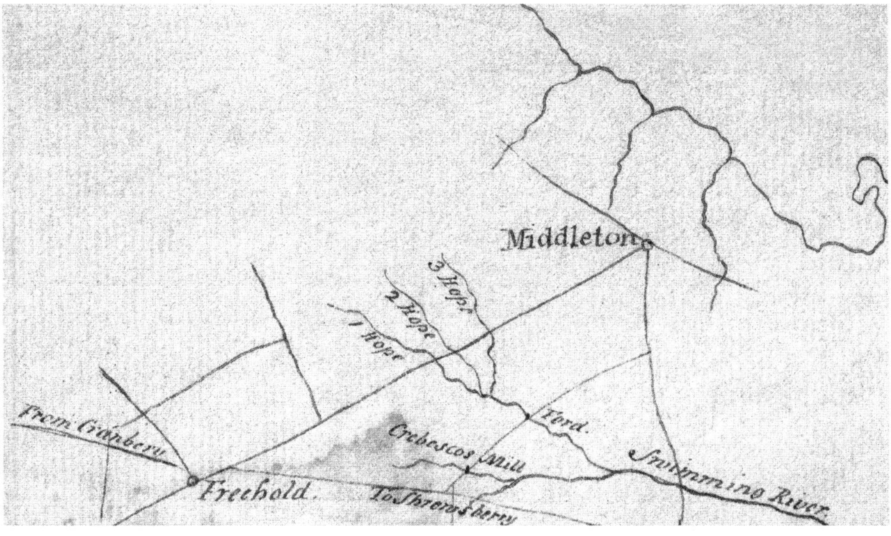

The intended British retreat from Freehold to Shrewsbury would have passed Hart's Tavern, south of Crebescos Mill (Probasco's) in top sketch. *Monmouth County Historical Association.*

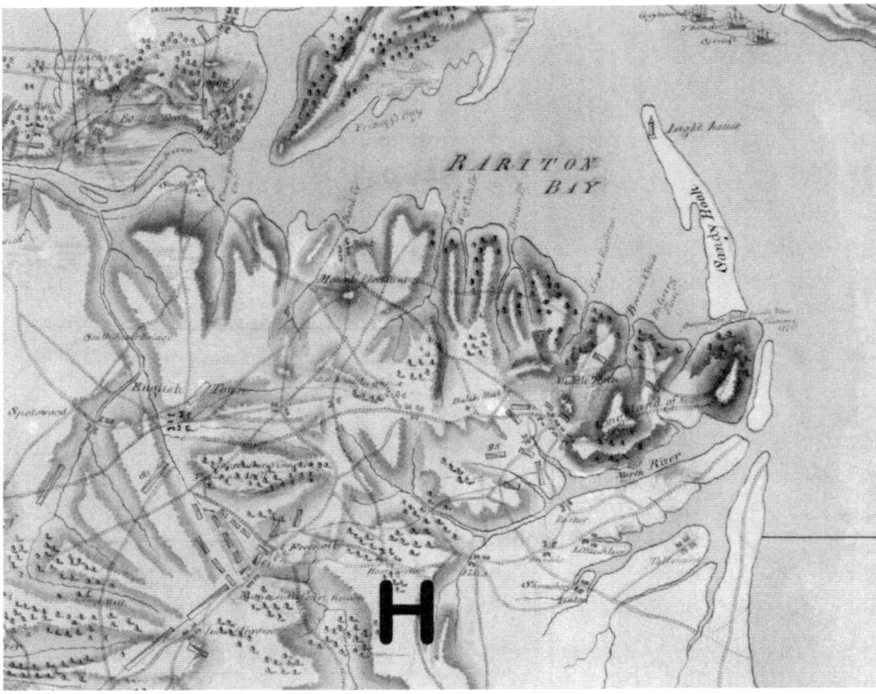

Above: Dutch Lane is the road from Freehold crossing the river north of Hart's Tavern (H). *Library of Congress.*

Left: Michael Field's grave in Colts Neck Memorial Park. *Rick Geffken.*

bravery." (The Battle at Monmouth Court House was militarily inconclusive, technically a draw. The Continental Army showed that it could hold its own against professional British soldiers. Washington's report claiming an American victory helped strengthen his position as commander-in-chief and encouraged rebels to believe that they were winning the war.)

Clinton said that he altered his original retreat plans at the urging of Major John Simcoe: "I also learned by other intelligence that detachments were moving in force on each of my flanks, and that a considerable corps was now advancing on the road toward Jews Town." Instead, Clinton redirected his main army to march north toward Middletown, avoiding a fight near Catherine Hart's tavern.

Around 5:00 a.m. on Monday morning, Joshua Huddy received an alert about the British movement from Freehold. The Second Division, commanded by Hessian General Wilhelm von Knyphausen, was escaping the battlefield in the darkness, and 1,500 wagons in a twelve-mile-long train were heading toward Nut Swamp in Middletown.

Huddy Engages the British

With a hastily mustered troop of fifteen militiamen, Huddy galloped toward Knyphausen. The exhausted British were struggling along the narrow Dutch Lane, slowed by the sandy hills of the Wickatonk Barrens. Huddy's men caught up with them at Vanderburg, two miles north of his Colts Neck home. They killed five British troops. Huddy pulled back from the attack after his men tried a reckless bayonet attack. Joseph Johnson recalled that he "fell in with Capt. Huddy at or near Colts Neck…engaged with a small party of the British horse…[and] helped to carry off a soldier who was cut by the sword of a horseman, he died." Michael Field was the slain man Johnson helped bury. They were both just nineteen years old.

British Cross Over to Sandy Hook

Clinton's main British forces reached the Navesink Hills on June 30. Simcoe's Queen's Rangers acted as a rear guard as long lines of men and equipment passed by Esek Hartshorne's house on the path down to a marshy area on

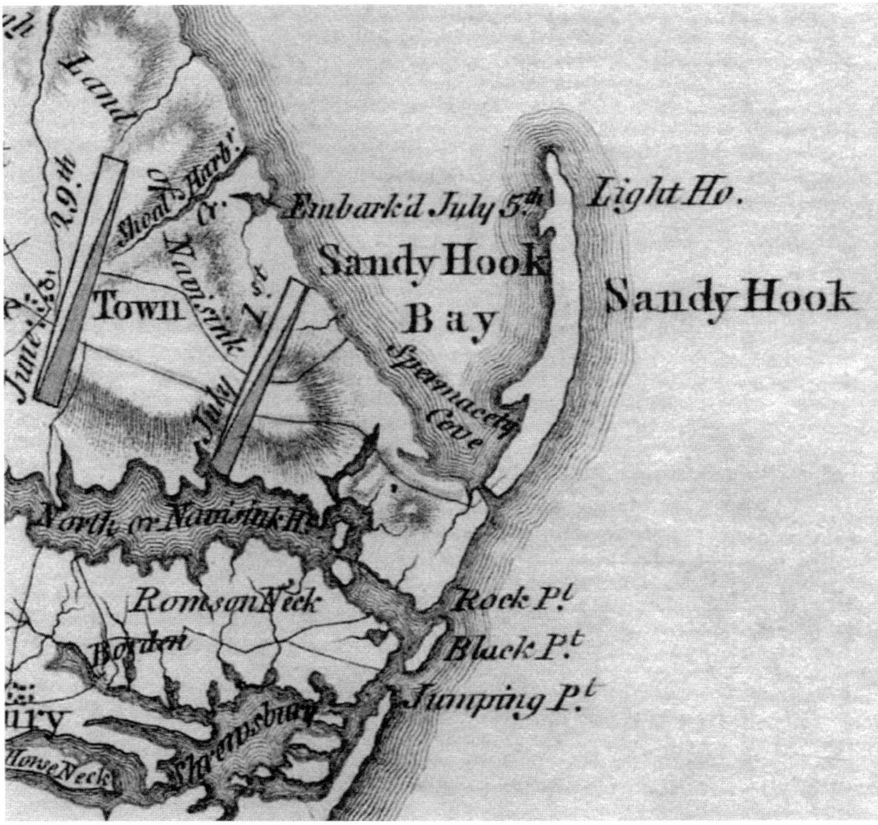

The British army left Navesink for Sandy Hook. *Public domain.*

the Shrewsbury River called Gravelly Point. The Queen's Rangers were the last troops to get across to Sandy Hook.

Because Tye was part of subsequent Queen's Rangers operations during 1779 and 1780, some assumed that he was also with them at Monmouth Court House. Tye might have been at Sandy Hook helping Clinton's troops during their evacuation, but historian Dr. David G. Martin told this author that he believes Tye was not at the actual battle.

Refugees did indeed transport the British wounded from Gravelly Point to Horseshoe Cove. But the majority went over at the narrowest section of the river about a mile south, between the mainland and Island Beach on a hastily constructed bridge made of small boats. Clinton's entire command was on Sandy Hook by July 5.

A British captain had this to say about the chaotic passage over the river:

> *Sunday 5th. July every thing embark'd but the Troops & a few horses. The army march'd between 5 & 6 from yr. respective ground by different roads to the point of the Highland that joins the Hook, & there is a Gut of water across the low Sandy part next the main, a Bridge of flat boats was made for the Troops to pass some embark'd on board of flat boats & rode off to their ships but the greatest part of the army crossed at the Bridge & march'd along the Hook towards the Light House & went off in flat boats to their ships in the afternoon; it was night before the whole got on board.—a great number of horses on Sandy Hook yet not embark'd into the Vessels that are to carry them up—the day cool, march about 6 miles in the woods before we came to the point & about 3 or 4 miles on Sandy Hook, deep sand—provision drawn on board a very irregular & ill managed Embarkation.*

Admiral Richard Howe's ships took the weary army to Staten Island and New York City.

Imperfect Memories of Colonel Tye

Assertions that Colonel Tye was at the Battle of Monmouth were based on statements from Revolutionary War veterans. When they applied for military pensions in the 1830s, several men mentioned supposed encounters with the famous Black Refugee. For instance, Freehold's Benjamin Vancleve equivocated in describing his "quite a smart engagement with a band of Refugees, headed, or <u>said to be</u>, by a negro called Colo. Tye" (author's emphasis).

Jacob Truax of Howell dictated his pension application in 1832:

> *He entered the militia service as a common militiaman in the fall of 1777 and continued in the service every other month till near the end of the war. And was in actual service upwards of two years in what was then called the monthly service in said county of Monmouth. That he was in a skirmish against Col. Tie* [sic] *near Eatontown in said county. The Refugees were commanded by this Col. Tie, a black man who was killed in that skirmish.*

Private Truax admitted that "by reason of old age and other consequent lapses of memory, he cannot swear particularly as to the precise length of his service." The seventy-one-year-old Truax mixed up his dates and was wrong about where Tye died.

On November 15, 1832, more than fifty years after the events, Sergeant Elisha Shepherd of Middletown wrote about his time in the war in a pension statement application:

> *The British Army retreated from Philadelphia through New Jersey when he was appointed a pilot to Col. Milans troop of horse who were pursuing the British Army, and after piloting them in safety to Middletown in Pleasant Valley was discharged and returned home to Solsbury* [Shrewsbury] *township in Monmouth County and again extended the service under the said Capt, Schanck and continued guarding the lines between the points above stated until taken prisoner by the Refugees under Col. Tye when he was taken to New York and put in the Provo or Hanging Jail which prison was under the direction of Capt. Cunningham, and continued confined in said prison to the end of the war.*

Jacob Shepherd testified that "himself and brother Elisha was taken prisoners by the British in the year Cornwallis the British general was taken."

Elisha Shepherd was eighty-two and Jacob seventy-six when they recollected their war years. Elisha might have been taken prisoner for the first time at the Battle of Monmouth, but Tye's Black Brigade was not there, nor was Tye even alive when General Cornwallis surrendered at Yorktown on October 19, 1781.

Old men's real or imagined encounters were confused by faulty memories and the fog of a war fought decades before. Their reminiscences became family gospel sometimes related to historians as truth.

Chapter 10

COLONEL TYE

Col. Tye, though guilty of having a skin darker than our own, yet was generally acknowledged to be about the most honorable, brave, generous and determined of the refugee leaders. Like our forefathers, he fought for his liberty, which our ancestors unfortunately refused to give him.
—Edwin Salter

In June 1779, General Henry Clinton issued a statement granting security within British lines to runaway slaves. In reaction, the *New-Jersey Journal* printed this mocking poem:

A Proclamation of late he sends
To thieves and rogues, who are his only friends
those he invites; all colors he attacks
but deference pays to Ethiopian Blacks.

Clinton's pledge, as had Lord Dunmore's proclamation four years before in Virginia, inspired "hundreds of enslaved New Jerseyans [to flee] their Patriot and Loyalist masters…to join the British forces in New York." It wasn't too long afterward that newspaper articles began identifying Colonel Tye as "one of Lord Dunmore's crew."

Tye's Early Raids?

Tye was probably perfecting his hit-and-run tactics before his reputation was established. The Refugees launched their boats at the small stream, which flowed south from the Sandy Hook Lighthouse, emptying into Horse Shoe Cove (see image on page 137). Earlier raids by Sandy Hook–based Refugees on rebel homes and farms in Shrewsbury and Middletown had all the characteristics of Tye's well-documented attacks.

In late spring 1778, seventy Skinner's Greens left Refugeetown for Middletown Point (Matawan). Named for the color of their uniforms, they operated from camps along the Jersey coast from Staten Island and Sandy Hook. The commander of these New Jersey Volunteers was a former New Jersey Attorney General Cortlandt Skinner.

The Greens' goal at the home of John Burrowes Sr. on May 27 was to interdict the produce and other goods he was supplying to the Continental Army. His son, Captain John Burrowes of the First New Jersey Regiment, was a secondary target. The Greens failed to destroy Burrowes' home but burned down his gristmills and transport vessels. Burrowes Sr. and four militia leaders were captured and several others killed or wounded. Captain Burrowes escaped.

Other such skirmishes bear Tye's style. Loyalists carried off seven prisoners at Tinton Falls in March 1779. Samuel Lippincott, a militiaman in Colonel Daniel Hendrickson's Third Regiment, remembered "defending our lives against the incursions and depredations of the Refugees and Tories, who at the time visited the settlements of Whigs, in predatory bands, for the purposes of plundering."

In May, two or three hundred Refugees invading Middletown were accused of "picarooning" (derived from the Spanish for rogue or pirate). "Four Negroes took" a prisoner from Monmouth County on June 6.

The *New Jersey Gazette* reported another instance: "On June 9th, a party of about fifty refugees (ex-slaves and loyalists) landed in Monmouth and marched to Tinton Falls undiscovered, where they surprised and carried off Col. Daniel Hendrickson, Col. Wyckoff, Capt. Chadwick, Captain McKnight and several privates of the militia, and also drove off sheep and horned cattle." A witness said that the fifty-plus Loyalist attackers "behaved like wild or mad men." Four otherwise unidentified Monmouth men were said to have guided the Refugees from Sandy Hook and back to Black Point after the attack.

Cortlandt Skinner. *Public domain.*

Lieutenant James Moody, a Loyalist from Little Egg Harbor, led the Tinton Falls assault. George Washington called him "that villain Moody." In his postwar memoirs, Moody named fifteen white Loyalists who were with him, referring to Black troops obliquely as "some guides." This was not an unusual omission since the British rarely named their fighting men of color in wartime reports. Moody did not cite Tye, but other accounts alleged that Hendrickson and Chadwick died while charging the Refugee colonel at Black Point.

The *New Jersey Gazette* ran a story about a July 11 incident: "About fifty Negroes and Refugees landed at Shrewsbury, and plundered the inhabitants of nearly eighty head of cattle, about 20 horses and a quantity of wearing apparel and household furniture. They also took William Brindley and Elihu Cook, two of the inhabitants." Historian Michael Adelberg believes, "This remarkably successful raid established Tye as Sandy Hook's most capable irregular leader."

Bold Audacity

During 1780, the Black Brigade's excursions were becoming increasingly bold. Lutheran minister Henry Muhlenberg observed, "The worst is to be feared from the irregular troops whom the so-called Tories have assembled…a regiment of Negroes, who are fitted for and inclined towards barbarities, are lack in human feeling and are familiar with every corner of the country."

With their intimate knowledge of the local geography, they guided Refugee raiding parties deeper into the Monmouth countryside. Their primary intent was to capture militia leaders, which they hoped would discourage rebels throughout the county. For two years, Tye was viewed as the leader of these marauders destroying homes and barns, stealing cattle and horses and taking everything they could carry.

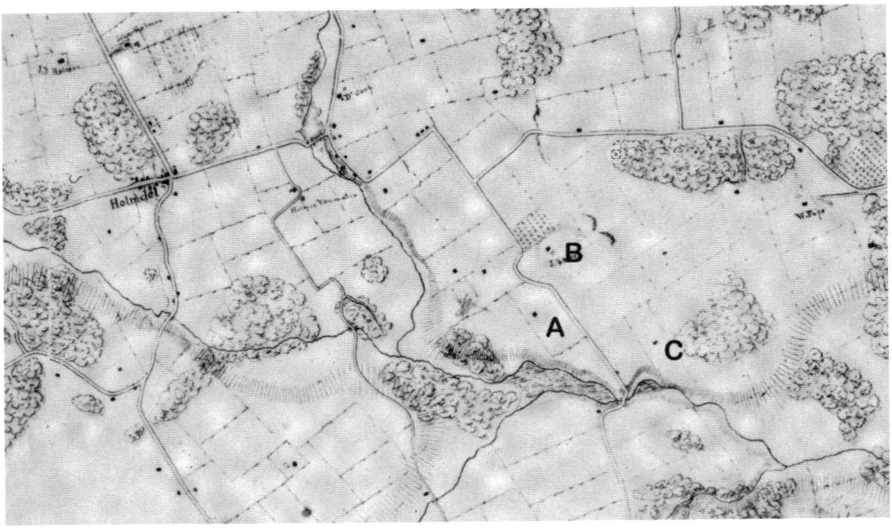

Colonel Tye captured Barnes Smock (A) and his cousin Gilbert VanMater (C) in Middletown. Colonel Johannes Smock (B) was taken two months later. *U.S. Coastal Survey Map.*

Samuel Lippincott recalled an incident involving Refugees. "On the night of the last of February, while in bed in his residence in Monmouth County, [his Shrewsbury home] was entered by five black refugees, who laid hands upon him and took him out of his bed. After having tied his hand behind him, they in company with several white Tories conveyed him and two other prisoners to Sandy Hook." Lippincott was imprisoned in the Sugar House for seven months before he was exchanged.

Samuel Lippincott was a Patriot Quaker who took up arms during the war. His first cousin, also a member of the Society of Friends, was the Loyalist Captain Richard Lippincott, who would eventually go head to head with an ex-Quaker, Joshua Huddy.

One of Tye's most dynamic raids occurred in the Pleasant Valley section of Middletown. A dozen miles from Sandy Hook, it was thought to be safe from Refugee attack. The rebel Smock family and their VanMater relatives were among the many Dutch farmers who plowed the rich lands between the village of Holmdel and the Willow Brook.

Hornets' Nest

The British called the area the Hornets' Nest because so many of their enemies operated from it. Militia Captain Barnes Smock's four-pounder cannon alerted his fellow militiamen whenever Tories conducted operations in and around Pleasant Valley. When it sounded, "Every man among the associated patriots, seized his rifle or musket, swung his powder horn and bullet pouch over his shoulders, and, often bare-footed, and in his shirt sleeves, would spring on his horse, and ride as fast as the horse could run, over to Capt. Smock's house." On the morning of Tye's raid, the cannon did not fire. It would stay permanently silent.

In the early daylight hours of June 9, 1780, Tye and his Refugees rode through Middletown Village and Nut Swamp on their way to Pleasant Valley. It was reported that "the sun one hour high.... Ty [*sic*], with his party of about 20 Blacks and Whites last Friday afternoon, took and carried off Prisoners, Capt. Barnes Smock and Gilbert VanMater, at the same time spiked up the iron four pounder at Capt. Smock's house, but took no

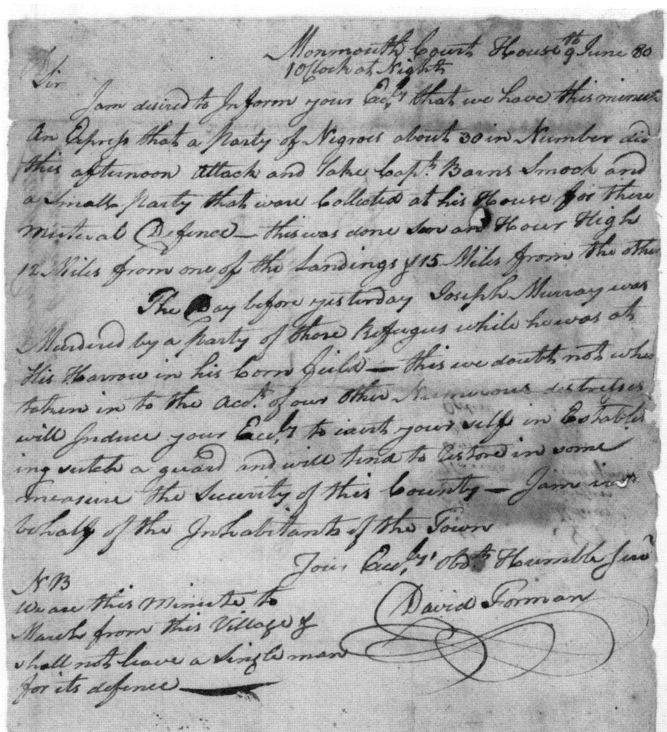

Monmouth Court House 9th June 80
10 o'Clock at Night

Sir

I am desired to Inform your Exc'y that we have this minute An Express that a Party of Negroes about 30 in Number did this afternoon attack and Take Capt. Barns Smock and a Small party that were Collected at his House for there mutual Defence — this was done Soon an Hour High 12 Miles from one of the Landings & 15 Miles from the other

The Day before yesterday Joseph Murray was Murdered by a party of those Refugees while he was at His Harrow in his Corn field — this we doubt not when taken in to the Acct. of our other Numerous distresses will Induce your Exc'y to exert your self in Establishing such a guard and will tend to restore in some measure the Security of this County — I am in behalf of the Inhabitants of the Town

Your Exc'y's Obdt. Humble Servt

David Forman

N.B.
We are this Minute to March from this Village & shall not leave a Single man for its defence —

David Forman's June 1780 letter to New Jersey Governor William Livingston. *Monmouth County Historical Association.*

ammunition. Two of the artillery horses and two of Capt. Smock's horses were taken off. The above mentioned Ty is a negro who bears the title of Colonel, and commands a motley crew at Sandy Hook."

Tye's men disabled the cannon by driving a steel spike into the cannon's touch hole (where the match ignites the propellant). David Forman wrote immediately to George Washington about the incident and another significant loss: "A party of Negroes about 30 in number did this afternoon attack and take Capt Barns Smock....The Day before yesterday Joseph Murray was Murdered by a party of those Refugees while he was at his Harrow in his Corn field." Curiously, Forman's letter omitted any mention of Tye.

The *New Jersey Journal* published a story about an attack on June 21, 1780, when "a party of the enemy, consisting of Ty [*sic*] with some 30 blacks, 30 Queen's Rangers, and 30 Refugee Tories, landed at Conascong [Union Beach]...went up to Mr. James Mott's, plundered his house... and carried off the following persons, viz., James Mott, Sen. Jonathan Pierce, James Johnson, Joseph Dorsett, William Blair, James Walling, Philip Walling, James Wall, Matthew Griggs, also several Negroes, and a great deal of stock." As the Refugees retreated, militiamen fought them in ferocious hand-to-hand combat.

Refugees and Retaliators

The Monmouth Militia's inability to prevent these frequent summer raids by the Refugees shook the entire population. In July, David Forman was elected chairman of the Monmouth Committee of Retaliation. The Retaliators' raison d'être was to seek vengeance on Loyalists by "Plundering's, Devastations, Kidnaping's [*sic*] and Even Murder." They were also not above settling personal grudges. The Retaliators operated every bit outside the law as did the Loyalists.

Predictably, the Refugees answered by targeting the Retaliators. On August 22, Tye allegedly captured Lieutenant Colonel John Smock and his son, Captain Hendrick Smock, a Retaliator board member. By then, whether or not he was involved, Tye was blamed anytime Black Refugees terrorized civilians or fought militiamen. His reputation grew so fearsome that few were eager to chase after him.

For a century before the war, harsh laws had tightly controlled slave behavior. They were forbidden to possess firearms, of course, but prohibited too from learning how to read and write. Enslavers were constantly worried that their Black chattel would pass messages back and forth with plans to rise up against them. Suddenly, it seemed that armed Black men were rampaging, murdering and stealing animals, food and supplies everywhere.

David Forman was worried enough to petition New Jersey Governor William Livingston for help. Livingston, whom Tories called "the Archfiend," declared martial law and sent a few hundred men from Burlington and Hunterdon Counties to reinforce Monmouth. Nonetheless, the Black Brigade would continue its intimidating attacks until the end of the war—for Tye, only three more months.

What Motivated Tye?

Titus/Tye left us no first-person accounts of his life. He was likely illiterate, kept so by the Corlies family. The few glimpses we have of him come from newspaper articles or letters written by his Revolutionary War opponents. Newspaper reports in those days were haphazard accounts, more or less true. Personal letters reflected the biases of their writers, of course. But these sources are all we have.

Tye spent the first twenty years of his life enslaved to a man he probably knew was his father. He was denied the privileges or recognition of his white siblings and was treated as less than human. The constant humiliations and the indignities left scars, physical and psychological. He grew up driving himself to overcome these liabilities, to earn dignity and respect.

Tye earned the honorary title "Colonel Tye" from his fellow Refugees for his inspiring leadership. He had developed an ability to make military plans, command other men and carry out successful operations. Still, he couldn't trust these white people clearly using him to achieve their goals, not his. He knew that his primary value to them was what he knew about Shrewsbury and the rebels. Tye believed that he could help the British win the war, but he must have wondered if they'd actually reward him with the freedom he was promised.

Both his allies and his enemies saw Colonel Tye through the lens of eighteenth-century racism. The British army never officially commissioned Black officers. Rebels exaggerated the fighting abilities of the Black warrior. Neither side saw him as the proud man he was.

Unanswered Questions

Despite what we know about Tye, at least two questions remain unanswered. Why are there no reports about attempts to exact revenge on John Corlies? Tye's Black Brigade was within easy striking distance of the Rumson Neck farm. They were at Black Point several times during the war. It's difficult to believe that Tye wouldn't look for Corlies. Revenge aside, wouldn't Tye have found a way to bring his mother, Sarah, over to Sandy Hook?

One plausible explanation is that the Corlies family had temporarily left Rumson (although John and his mother, Zilpha, remained on property tax lists during the war). John Corlies was in Burlington during the fall of 1776. After he stole George Washington's letters, he knew that the authorities were looking for him in Shrewsbury. He'd have a good reason to hide somewhere else with his wife, two young children and his slaves. Corlies died in November 1786, but there is no grave marker for him in the family plot at the Rumson Burying Ground. It's possible he never returned, thwarting any reprisal from his former slave, Titus.

Chapter 11

TOMS RIVER CONNECTION

A good privateersman was a mixture of gall and guts, of bluff, bravery, and good seamanship, with a fair slice of luck thrown in.
—Jack Coggins

Three or four years fighting the British would make you a marked man. His Majesty's troops and the irregular Refugees would be threats, but your neighbors and tavern customers posed risks too. Loyalist civilians, acting as a kind of informal spy network, could report on your personal habits, how and where you operated and when you might be home. The longer you fought for your new nation's independence, the greater the chance you'd lose your own. You'd be running out of safe places to minimize your exposure.

Huddy to the Navy

Facing this dilemma in 1780, Joshua Huddy thought he found a solution, assisting the nascent Continental Navy as a privateer. Commanding a privateer would bring protection and financial rewards. During the war, all manner of privateering vessels—brigantines, schooners and sloops, disguised to look like merchant ships—harassed and interrupted British shipping up and down the Jersey coast. Figuring out how to inveigle a naval commission was, literally, right in Huddy's wheelhouse.

Huddy, touting his maritime experience on the Delaware River, convinced David Forman to get him a new assignment. While the claim was technically true, Huddy's nautical skills were probably as rusty as an old anchor. Black David didn't need too much persuading. He loved Huddy's derring-do, initiative and vengeful ethos, reflections of how he saw himself.

Forman had organized a vigilante group whose members swore to protect one another from Loyalists. The Committee of Retaliation settled personal disputes, stole private property and murdered whoever they pleased, all in the name of liberty.

Black Snake

David Forman used his influence to free Huddy from the tightening noose of relentless Loyalist pressure. Forman was one of many top-echelon American Patriots acquainted with the Randolph family of Upper Freehold. George Washington knew Benjamin Randolph, a well-known Philadelphia cabinetmaker who made crates for the Continental Army and rented lodgings to the American general after the British abandoned the city. Thomas Jefferson wrote the Declaration of Independence on a portable writing desk that Randolph crafted specifically for him.

Benjamin's oldest brother, James Randolph, was a wealthy Toms River owner of timber mills, lumber operations and saltworks. Like so many other entrepreneurs, enslaved people largely powered his businesses. Their attitude toward freeing slaves was represented in the *New Jersey Gazette*:

> *At this time when many parts of the state in the neighbourhood of the enemy are laid waste and rendered desolate by the ravages of that army, and many families driven from their lands depend in a great measure on the labour of slaves for their livelihood, it would be unreasonable to deprive them of their only support.*

Daniel Randolph, an attorney and justice of the peace, was as patriotic as his brothers. He sent a request to the legislature asking for relief at Toms River:

> *Your subscribers have ever since the war exerted themselves for the Liberties of America and are still willing to do all in their powers to carry the point, but finding our strength insufficient, beg leave to inform your Honours that*

NAVAL RECORDS OF THE REVOLUTION. 241

1780 Aug. 18 **Black Snake.** Pennsylvania boat. Gun: 1. Crew: 14. Bond: $20,000. Master: Joshua Huddy [Philadelphia?].

Bonders: Benjamin Davis jr., Philadelphia. Thomas Sliter, Philadelphia.
Owners: James Randolph. Joshua Huddy & Co.
Witness: James Trimble.

Huddy and Randolph owned *Black Snake*. *Naval Records of the Revolution.*

> *the enemies of the United States…so carry on a clandestine trade contrary to the laws of the state…and the inhabitants of Toms River, in said town, have been frequently threatened to be plundered and their houses raised, & after the militia are not very numerous…therefore we beg…that an Act be passed for forming a volunteer company to assist of about thirty men properly officered & provisioned.*

When David Forman suggested that one of his militia captains had exemplary qualifications, James Randolph considered partnering with Huddy. These influential rebels had common purpose beyond their beef with the British—they were not above enriching themselves with the spoils of war.

Forman's connections paid off in mid-August when Huddy and James Randolph were granted a letter of marque, basically a license for legalized piracy in an armed cargo-carrier. Of the estimated seven hundred American privateers operating against British shipping, Huddy was one of only four from New Jersey sanctioned by the fledgling national government.

The Continental Congress, no doubt at Washington's urging, specified Huddy's duties:

> *The Condition of this Obligation is such, That whereas Joshua Huddy, Master and Commander of the Armed boat called Black Snake belonging to James Randolph, Joshua Huddy and Company mounting one swivel gun, and navigated by fourteen men, who hath applied for and received a Commission, bearing date with these Presents, licencing* [sic] *and authorizing him to fit out and set forth the said Armed boat in a warlike manner, and by and with the said Armed boat and the officers and crew thereof, by force of arms to attack, subdue, seize and take all ships and other*

> *vessels, goods, wares and merchandizes, belonging to the Crown of Great-Britain, or any of the subjects thereof.*

During the Revolution, at least three other warships were named *Black Snake*, perhaps inspired by Benjamin Franklin's famous prewar image urging the British colonies to unite. In April 1780, privateer Captain William Marriner sailed a captured brigantine of the same name to Toms River. Maybe James Randolph liked the name so much he appropriated it for his new vessel.

Risk-taking privateers made quick money. Salaries of sixteen dollars per month per man—twice as much as what ordinary Continental Navy sailors earned—attracted all kinds of rogue seamen. Huddy and Randolph induced a crew of the *Black Snake* with generous pay and the promise of splitting proceeds from the sale of captured British vessels and cargos.

Black Snake needed bonding to ensure compliance with privateer laws. Financier Benjamin Davis, one of the men who put up the money, had served in the Philadelphia Cavalry with Benjamin Randolph.

James Randolph's four-hundred-acre plantation called Cove Place was on the north side of the Toms River. His huge spread was ideally situated for

Benjamin Franklin's *Pennsylvania Gazette* printed this image in 1754. *Public domain.*

privateering operations. It was just across the bay from Cranberry Inlet, a narrow and shallow passage that allowed small boats to pass over its bar and prevented large British warships from entering.

Black Snake's primary mission was to engage with British merchant ships, but stepped with a mast and sails, it could also get Randolph's salt to Philadelphia. After the British left, ships had an easier time going up the Delaware with food and vital staples. Joshua Huddy knew the river as well as anyone.

One historian described the operation of small privateering boats this way:

> *Silently, with muffled oars, this little craft stole across the bay…* [the captain] *ran his little boat quietly under the stern of the* [brig]. *His men swarmed noiselessly over her counter, seized the unsuspecting lookout, secured the entrance to cabin and forecastle, thus imprisoning the sleeping crew below, battened down the hatches, got sail on the brig, catted her anchor, and stood out to sea—all this without creating alarm or suspicion.*

Details about the *Black Snake* are scanty, but it must have been a whaleboat. These long and narrow rowboats made "with both ends sharp and raking" were steered with an oar or a fixed rudder. It was lightly armed, fitted with an easily hidden swivel gun to protect its fourteen-man crew.

As exciting as this new venture was for Joshua Huddy, he never got to plunder or profit from it. A few weeks after he got his letter of marque, he was home awaiting an assignment when his Colts Neck house was surrounded by a Loyalist patrol.

Chapter 12

BLACK POINT, THE BACKSTORY

On Sunday Night a Party of Refugees came as high as Colt's Neck and took off Capt. Huddy with the Loss of one of the Party killed there, & it is said Colo. Tye being wounded in the Wrist.
—Nathaniel Scudder

After the British army left Monmouth County, the Revolutionary conflict deteriorated into fierce guerrilla warfare. Irregulars on both sides used ambushes, sabotage and surprise strikes to rattle their opponents.

Colonel Tye and the Black Brigade struck at random, inflicting casualties, taking prisoners and confiscating food, cattle and supplies of all kinds. Anytime Black fighters assaulted rebels or their sympathizers, Tye was accused of leading them.

Joshua Huddy's unpredictability aggravated British Loyalists. He'd commanded an artillery unit and then mounted a cavalry attack against the retreating British army. In the late summer of 1780, Tories learned that he would soon take up privateering. They decided to put an end to his assaults once and for all. Tipped off that Huddy was home in Colts Neck, they drew up a quick plan to capture the obnoxious rebel in a pre-dawn siege.

On September 9, Tye was selected to guide Lieutenants Josiah Parker and William Hewlet (both from Shrewsbury) and twenty men on a mission to take Huddy when they thought he'd be asleep and alone. Black and white Refugees rowed to the mainland to meet with friendlies waiting at Black Point with horses and wagons. They rode through the night, hunkering down in the woods near Abraham Probasco's Mill, one mile from Huddy's house and Hart's Tavern.

Siege

Huddy was usually accompanied by a small detachment of militiamen. On this particular night, he allowed his guards to visit their families. By a stroke of luck, they left a few weapons with Huddy.

Around four o'clock in the morning, the Refugees snaked one by one down the Mine Brook from Probasco's. Cutting off escape routes, they took up positions around their quarry's home. Huddy was startled awake by rocks shattering his windows, quickly followed with shouts: "Huddy, we've got you now. Will you come out?"

His answer was an immediate shot fired from the second floor. Seconds later, a muzzle flash illuminated a downstairs window. The besiegers returned fire from hiding places behind fences, the corners of the tavern and weed-covered ditches. Some were hit as they maneuvered for closer vantage points.

Surprised to see several Refugees picked off, Tye thought Huddy had ten men with him. Cursing the intelligence he'd relied on against his better instincts, he was nonetheless confident that the bastardly bunch would run out of ammunition before too long if his comrades kept up their fire.

Thump! Huddy's aim was true. A sharp round hitting Tye's wrist threw him back a step. He dropped his splintered musket and then wrapped a piece of his shirt around the wound. The makeshift bandage turned bright red.

Casualties mounting, the Refugees had no idea that Huddy was the only one shooting at them, nor that he was assisted by a young girl, still in her nightclothes. Lucretia Emmons was later described as Huddy's slave, a "colored" servant girl or even his mistress, but she was probably just his white housekeeper. Although some reports said that Huddy's wife, Catherine, was there too, it's unlikely since the couple were estranged at the time.

Was Lucretia as devoted to the rebel cause as Huddy? Maybe, but for years afterward, Mrs. Lucretia Chambers was never shy about relating her heroic actions during the famous siege, assuring listeners of her significant role. She actually did earn the fame that came her way. During the siege, Lucretia was uncommonly brave for teenage girl, crawling behind Huddy, room to room, front to back, upstairs and down. Every time he shot, she reloaded the weapons and then dashed with him, head down, to another window. The deception lasted twenty minutes or so, confusing the Refugees until they changed tactics—they'd burn the buggers out.

When a raider ran up with a lighted torch, Huddy knew that he had only two options: surrender or incineration. The front door was ablaze

Above: Marker near the site of Joshua Huddy's house in Colts Neck today. *Rick Geffken.*

Opposite: Nathaniel Scudder's September 1780 letter to his son Joseph. *New Jersey Historical Society.*

when he heard, "Quarters!" The smart choice was to take the offer to give up and be taken prisoner. From a second-floor window, Huddy waved his musket, a piece of white bed linen on the barrel, yelling, "Put out the fire, we yield."

The Refugees threw buckets of water at the door and barged through. Shocked that only two people had held them at bay, several argued vociferously for killing Huddy on the spot, promises be damned. They were furious, bent on revenging Tye's injury. Talked down from instant retribution, they reluctantly acceded. For spite, they refused Huddy's request to change out of his nightclothes. They had no use for a servant girl and let Lucretia go free. They couldn't resist taking some of Huddy's cows and sheep as prizes, an unwise decision (see chapter 1).

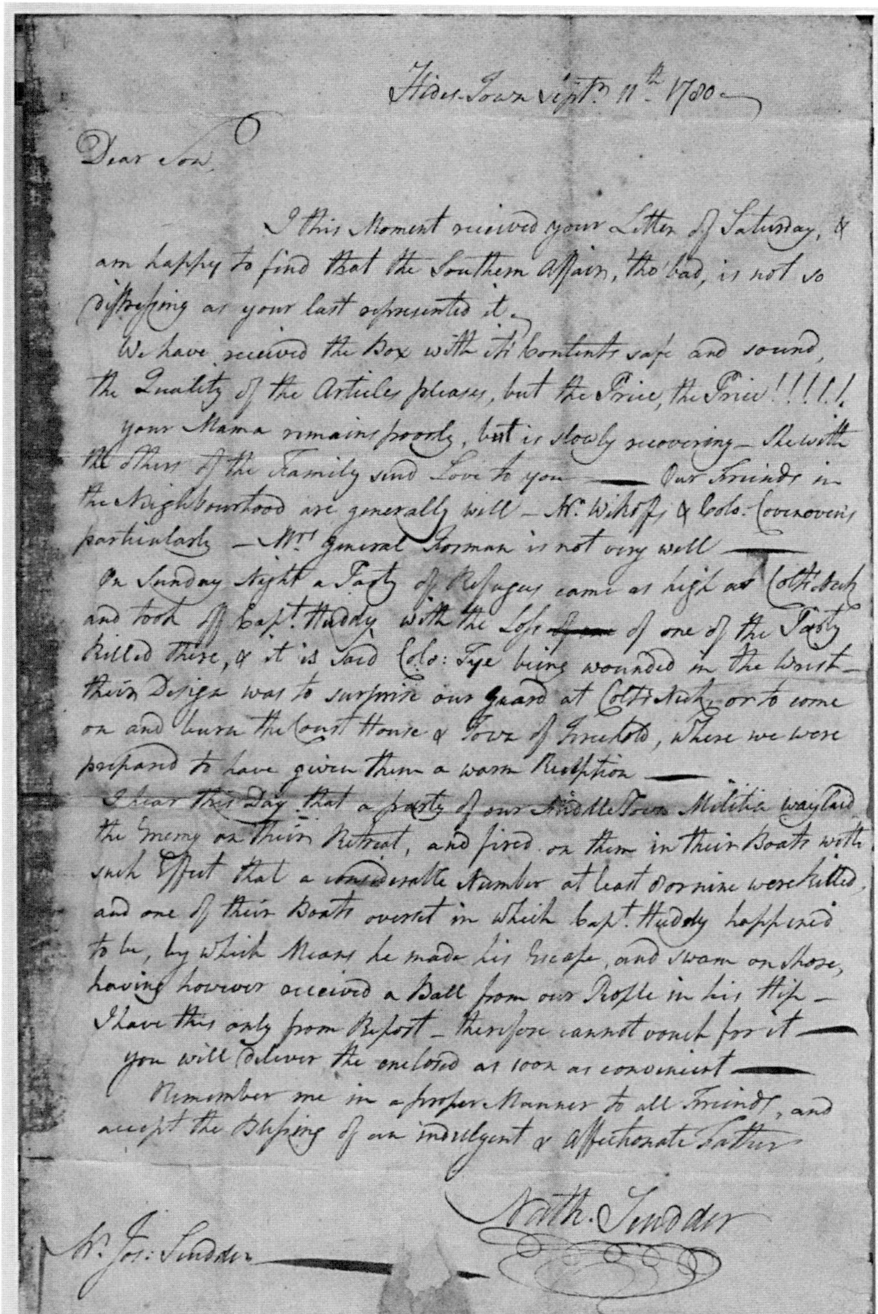

Hides-Town Septr. 11th 1780

Dear Son

I this Moment received your Letter of Saturday, & am happy to find that the Southern Affair, tho bad, is not so distressing as your last represented it.

We have received the Box with its Contents safe and sound, the Quality of the Articles pleases, but the Price, the Price!!!!!

Your Mama remains poorly, but is slowly recovering — She with the others of the Family send Love to you — Our Friends in the Neighbourhood are generally well — Mr. Wikoff & Colo. Covenhoven's particularly — Mrs. General Forman is not very well —

On Sunday Night a Party of Refugees came as high as Colts Neck and took off Capt. Huddy with the Loss of one of the Party killed there, & it is said Colo: Tye being wounded in the Wrist — their Design was to surprise our Guard at Colts Neck, or to come on and burn the Court House & Town of Freehold, where we were prepared to have given them a warm Reception —

I hear this Day that a party of our Middletown Militia waylaid the Enemy on their Retreat, and fired on them in their Boats with such Effect that a considerable Number at least 8 or nine were killed, and one of their Boats overset in which Capt. Huddy happened to be, by which Means he made his Escape, and swam on shore, having however received a Ball from our People in his Hip — I have this only from Report — therefore cannot vouch for it —

You will deliver the enclosed as soon as convenient —

Remember me in a proper Manner to all Friends, and accept the Blessing of an indulgent & affectionate Father

Nath. Scudder

Mr. Jos: Scudder

Huddy Rescued

Within days, Colonel Nathaniel Scudder wrote about the incident to his son Joseph. His letter was the earliest report of Colonel Tye's wound. Historians of the Revolution sourced Scudder's letter to speculate that Tye succumbed to tetanus (others said lockjaw). The idea was not a far-fetched diagnosis in an age before modern antibiotics when severe injuries might result in terminal infections. Scudder, a Freehold physician, made no such claim. In fact, he wrote that he couldn't be certain of particulars because he wasn't a firsthand witness to the events:

> *Dear Son, On Sunday Night a Party of Refugees came as high as Colt's Neck and took off Capt. Huddy with the Loss of one of the Party killed there, & it is said Colo. Tye being wounded in the Wrist. Their Design was to surprise our Guard at Colts Neck, or to come on and burn the Court House & Town of Freehold, where we were prepared to have given them a warm Reception. I hear this Day that a party of our Middle Town Militia waylaid the Enemy on their Retreat, and fired on them in their Boats with such Effect that a considerable Number at least 8 or nine were killed, and one of their Boats overset in which Capt. Huddy happened to be, by which Means he made his Escape, and swam on Shore, having however received a Ball from our People in his thigh. I have this only from Report, therefore* [I] *cannot vouch for it.*

Colonel Tye, MIA

One month after the dramatic events at Black Point, the *Pennsylvania Packet* published an account "taken from Captain Huddy himself." The article contained ambiguous and contradictory details allowing for different interpretations. Huddy, or the reporter, confirmed that the "brave Negro Tye" was wounded and also that "six militia men…killed the refugee Commander." It's unclear which commander was dispatched because the article reported that "Refugees and Negroes [were] under the command of Lieuts. Josiah Parker and William Hewlet." If Tye wasn't killed by musket fire or didn't die from tetanus, a look at the two sources suggest another outcome.

When the shots broke out, several Refugee boats capsized, spilling dead and wounded into the water. It was every man for himself, some clinging to the overturned boats and others grasping for anything floating. Those who could swim thrashed and kicked, diving to avoid incoming musket fire.

Huddy was inadvertently hit by a militia round. He fell or jumped overboard, swimming back to shore. Worried that he'd be mistaken for one of his captors, he yelled between sputtering breaths, "I am Huddy, I am Huddy!" Ensign William Vincent ordered his six Salem militiamen to cease fire. Huddy was dragged up onto the beach and moved into the wood line for protection and a quick patch-up. His rescuers let him rest for a bit, keeping an eye on the Refugees until they no longer posed a threat.

Years later, John Eldridge of Middletown regaled his grandchildren with a story of his personal heroism. Eldridge claimed that he was the militiaman who ran into the water to pull Huddy to safety, being greeted with, "Hello, Captain Eldridge, you are just in time." Eldridge, a militia private who had not mentioned his role in Huddy's rescue in his 1833 government pension application, was probably exaggerating his Revolutionary service.

Huddy, too busy saving himself, probably had no idea what happened to Tye at Black Point. My conjecture is that Tye's injured wrist made it difficult for him to swim the fast-moving waters of the Shrewsbury. Each stroke brought more pain. He couldn't duck the militia rounds pouring in on him. Some found their mark. Exhausted, Tye slipped under the water and drowned. His body was swept away by currents. He may have breathed his last not far from where his life had begun.

If Refugees did find Tye's remains, they may have buried him on Sandy Hook. The British were typically scrupulous in recording the deaths of their own troops, though not necessarily for Black guides. We have no burial report, although we'd expect none if his body was never recovered. After September 1780, there were no credible accounts of Colonel Tye leading Refugees (the Black Brigade continued operations under different leaders). We have no after-action reports from Lieutenant Josiah Parker or Lieutenant William Hewlet, possibly because the officers were reluctant to file anything about a failed mission. Colonel Tye's final resting place, if he had one, is one more part of his legend.

After Black Point

Joshua Huddy's harrowing capture at Colts Neck and narrow escape at Black Point dashed his hopes for a lucrative privateering career. No naval records or newspaper articles have been found showing he ever put to sea to challenge British shipping.

Huddy faced yet another dilemma. Since British Loyalists knew where he lived and would surely be on the lookout for his return, Huddy couldn't go back to Colts Neck. He spent the next sixteen months elsewhere, sheltering with militia friends, possibly even David Forman.

When his estranged wife realized that he couldn't risk living at their Colts Neck home, Catherine and her son Jacob Hart moved back into the house and tavern. Huddy was not the kind of man to let that insult to his dignity go unanswered.

In November 1780, Huddy sued the attorney John Longstreet in the New Jersey Supreme Court. He alleged that the Freehold attorney and criminal court judge had unjustly seized "three horses, two cows, eight hogs, twenty bushels of Indian corn, and several acres of other grain still in the ground, five feather beds & sundry other articles of household furniture." Why would Joshua Huddy sue Longstreet?

When Levy Hart died in 1775, his widow, Catherine, formally renounced her role as executor of her husband's will "in favor of John Longstreet, Esq.," thus giving Longstreet the right to administer the Hart property. Catherine's daughter Rebecca Hart and John's son, Elias Longstreet, witnessed the document. Once Huddy vacated the Colts Neck property, Longstreet counseled Catherine Huddy, who was living on his Freehold farm, to go home.

Despite Longstreet's opinion, Huddy believed that he was the rightful owner of the Colts Neck estate and brought the attorney to court. Huddy had a point. The colonial doctrine of coverture disadvantaged women, stripping them of legal identity. Married women owned nothing, their husbands everything.

The New Jersey Supreme Court decided for Huddy—the former Hart property was his. Sheriff David Forman would enforce the court's ruling. However, if Huddy was able to recover some of his goods and chattel, it's unlikely that he ever lived in Colts Neck again. From 1781 onward, Shrewsbury records show Jacob Hart and his mother, Catherine, owing taxes on the fifty-acre farm. There are no further entries for Joshua Huddy.

Joshua Huddy created another problem for himself in March 1781. Continental Army Private Richard Burdge accused Huddy of stealing his "Riding Chair or Chaise" (a small, two-wheeled horse carriage) worth thirty pounds. Huddy's defence was something along the lines of finding the chair he thought was abandoned. He lost the case and was convicted of trespass and fined fifty pounds.

Once he got through the year's hectic early months, Joshua Huddy avoided trouble, as well as the hands of his British Loyalist enemies—for the duration of 1781 at least.

Chapter 13

AN ENDLESS CYCLE OF REVENGE

Blood shall flow for blood.
—William Cunningham

More than one hundred Revolutionary War battles and skirmishes were fought in the farms and fields of Monmouth, more than in any other New Jersey county. Families divided themselves into Loyalist or rebel factions. One-time friends and neighbors took lethal aim at each other from opposite sides of the conflict. Innocent civilians were kidnapped, tortured and killed based on innuendos or lies. In this atmosphere of eye-for-an-eye reciprocal justice, a cycle of hangings led to the most infamous necktie party of the entire war at an obscure beach called Gravelly Point.

Tit for Tat

In September 1778, Stephen Edwards left Shrewsbury for New York. He joined the Associated Loyalists, a network of Loyalist spies and guerrilla fighters organized by the former royal governor of New Jersey, William Franklin (the illegitimate son of Benjamin). The Associators claimed they were proud of their "Excesses, Barbarities or Irregularities, contrary to the acknowledged Laws of War as practiced by civilized Nations."

Monmouth County Loyalists and rebels terrorized each other during the Revolution. *National Park Service.*

Colonel George Taylor, the former militiaman turned Loyalist commander, gave Edwards written orders to return to Monmouth County as a spy. Edwards was assigned to gather intelligence on rebel leaders, meeting locations and anything else of value.

During a time when anything new or odd aroused suspicion, Edwards's sudden reappearance at his father's house in Eatontown was noted and passed along to militia Captain Jonathan Forman, a cousin of Black David Forman.

At midnight on a Saturday in November, Captain Forman and Joshua Huddy with a few militiamen roused the sleeping Edwards and his wife. Stephen was dressed in Abigail's nightclothes, a disguise that fooled no one. Taylor's orders were found under the bed in a pile of rumpled clothes.

Edwards was rushed to Freehold for a quick hearing in front of David Forman and Huddy. Verdict: guilty of spying. On Monday morning, Edwards was taken to "the corner of Daniel Barcalow's woods, the noted hanging place" where dozens of captured Loyalists met their end.

Edwards's parents, Webley and Margaret, were at the Monmouth jail the same morning to visit Stephen. Instead, they went home with his remains, appalled by how quickly judgment was passed and sentence rendered. Their grief was all the more acute because the Edwards and Forman families were friendly and distantly related through marriage. The war in Monmouth County had become increasingly uncivil.

Loyalists played the same deadly game fixing on real or suspected enemies. In March 1780, Captain Richard Lippincott, his cousin Philip White, Colonel Tye and some Black Brigade Refugees targeted a Shrewsbury father and son. John Russell Sr. was near seventy, too old to soldier but still scrappy enough to wield a musket at the first sign of trouble threatening him and his wife, Hannah. His daughter-in-law Louise was staying with them, while John Jr. patrolled with the militia. On this night, twenty-four-year-old John was home with his family.

As soon as they heard the rustling outside, the Russells readied their weapons, holding fire until the attackers burst through the front door. Noise, smoke and shouting punctuated the air as shots were exchanged. Men on both sides were killed, including the elder Russell. A Russell grandson was hit five times, but the young boy somehow survived.

John Jr. lay bleeding on the floor, feigning death. A Refugee attacker suspected the fakery and took aim to finish him off. Sneering that the rebel would die soon enough, Lippincott knocked the man's weapon up. The round hit the ceiling. Satisfied that they'd done enough damage, the raiders left for another mission.

While the frantic Louise bandaged his wounds, the unbowed John Jr. said, "Ducky, bring me a glass of whiskey, I'll come out all right yet." When he did recover, John Russell carried a smoldering grudge along with his scars.

Philip White Killed

In March 1782, Philip White, his brother Aaron, Clayton Tilton and three other Loyalists sailed down the Shrewsbury River from Refugeetown to Long Branch. When word reached the Sons of Liberty, John Russell Jr. was one of a dozen men from the rebel resistance group to respond. The Sons chased the intruders to the marshy Raccoon Island. After a short fight at Snag Swamp on Manhasset Creek, the outnumbered Loyalists gave up on condition they'd be taken to the Monmouth Jail and held for a fair trial.

John Russell, John North and William Borden guarded Philip White on the way to Freehold. Russell's seething memory of his father's death was more than enough for him to issue shoot-to-kill orders if White attempted to escape. Aaron White, under a separate group of guards, rode behind his brother. When they reached Colts Neck, Aaron's group galloped ahead of Philip's.

What happened next along the Burlington Road was spun into wildly competing accusations. The rebel perspective, the more accurate version, had it that a few miles short of Freehold, the guards stopped to water their horses by a little bridge over a mill stream. Philip White looked around and realized that they were coming up on "the hanging place." Thinking that he'd been lied to, he panicked, darting on a desperate run for the fence line between the homes of Loyalists Daniel Grandin and Samuel Leonard. White dodged and weaved through a field, heading for a tree line.

Borden fired a round that went through White's back, exited at his breast and knocked him to the ground. Borden and North raced their horses toward the runner, shouting, "If you give up, you shall have quarters yet." Somehow White found the strength to get up and stagger toward a bog.

Overtaking the bleeding White, Borden butted him with a carbine. North jumped off his horse and struck White across the face with his sword. "I'm a dead man" were Philip White's last words. Borden and North carried his limp body back to a wagon. Philip's horrified brother Aaron watched the entire scene from the road.

Conversely, Loyalists said that Russell was "highly exasperated against the prisoner," such that he and "[the guards] pricked him with their swords,

Nearing Freehold, Philip White fled where the mill stream (*far right*) crossed the Old Burlington Road (X). *Public domain.*

forcing him to run, and cruelly murdered him." And which prominent Patriot did they blame for the diabolical deed? Joshua Huddy, of course.

The fabrication insisted that Huddy "had taken a certain Refugee by the name of Philip White and after carrying him five or six miles, cut off his arms, broke both his legs, pulled out one of his eyes, then damned him and bid him run" before cruelly murdering him. The rumor was believable enough—supposed depredation happened within the militia captain's area of operations, along a road near his home and tavern.

To make the sordid affair sound grislier, it was alleged that Philip White's mutilated body was hung up at the jail for public view and that his sister, Susannah, was denied permission to recover the body before it was dumped in a shallow makeshift grave in the jail yard. None of this grotesquery was true.

David Forman testified that he'd seen no mutilations on Philip White's body, just "the gunshot wound on the breast, also the cuts of a sword on his face. At that time, the corpse appeared to be laid with as much decency as could be." Tories scoffed at what they believed to be Black David's meaningless drivel, sure that his words were part of a cover-up.

Eyewitness Aaron White testified that Huddy had no part in Philip's murder—to no avail.

Chapter 14

THE BLOCKHOUSE DISASTER

He was continually and everywhere hunting the Tories, the British spies from New York, the pine robbers, or all combined; and they in turn seeking his life, and hunting him like "a partridge of the mountains."
—*The Monmouth Democrat*

The little village of Toms River sat near the head of the river from which it took its name. With fewer than a dozen dwellings and shops, and a single tavern, the town itself was not as important as its shallow harbor. Small trading vessels took advantage of easy access to other coastal ports. Not surprisingly, smugglers turned Toms River into an active privateering center.

James Randolph

James Randolph's timber operations and the Pennsylvania Salt Works were downriver, on the inland side of Flat Bay Sound (Barnegat Bay). The Cranberry Inlet, a short sail across the bay, allowed easy access to and from the Atlantic Ocean.

Before the Revolutionary War, the colonies imported salt from Europe. After 1776, Americans had to manufacture their own salt. Besides its preservative and medicinal qualities, salt was a key ingredient in making

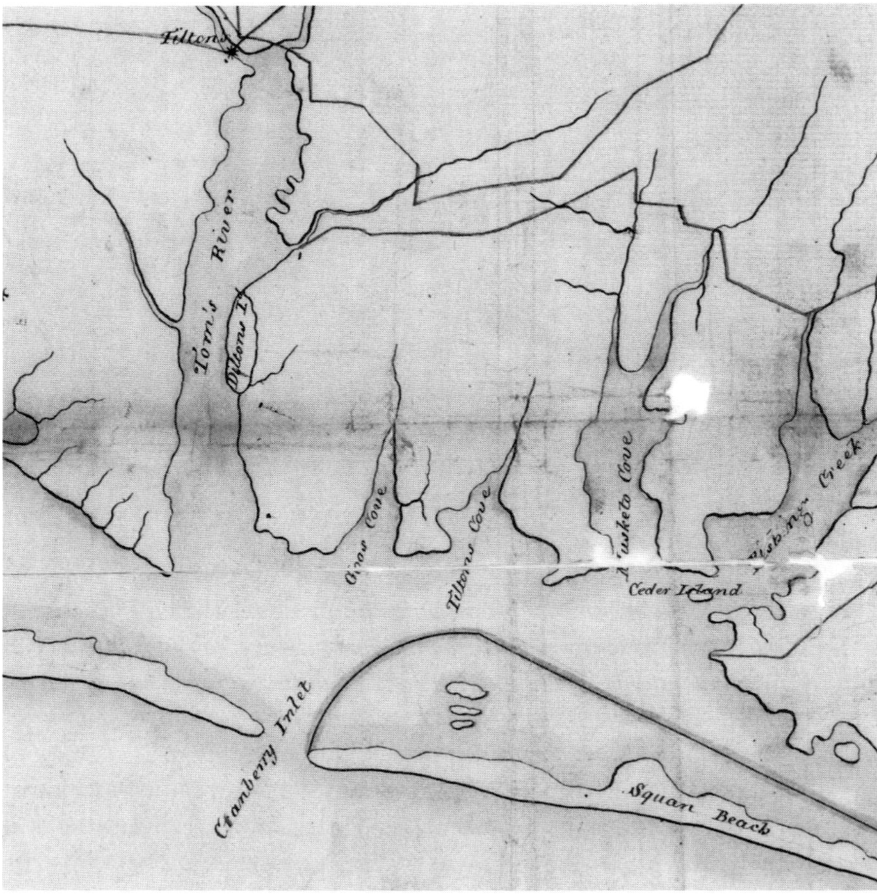

gunpowder. The Pennsylvania Salt Works, largest along the Jersey shore, consisted of five hundred acres of salt meadow near Coates Point and Shelter Cove. It was a perfect site—the rise and fall of the tides left a salty residue, easy to extract. The saltworks consisted of a 169-foot-by-29-foot boiling house "with a 50 ft. by 20 ft. stove, two drying houses, a kitchen, stable, lime house, blacksmith shop, and windmill-powered water pumps."

As early as February 1777, the manager of the saltworks reported the area's vulnerabilities:

> *A small sloop or tender came into this inlet, manned Chiefly by Tories who went on board a sloop belonging to Mr. James Randolph & Others, with the intent to take her Out; but not being able to accomplish that, plundered her of What they Could and went off on seeing a small party of Militia coming down from the head of the river…the Militia of this part of the*

Opposite: James Randolph's plantation was north of Toms River and opposite Cranberry Inlet. *Library of Congress.*

Above: The Pennsylvania Salt Works. *Collection of the Ocean County Historical Society.*

> *Country are by no means Calculated for the defence thereof; for more than half of them are Tories, and the rest but little better. I am of Opinion that if this part of the Country is to be defended it must be by Continental troops, who know their duty…also one or two Gallys to protect this and the neighboring inlets. I am in expectation of another Vissett from them.*

The Tories indeed returned just a few days later, stealing the sloop's rigging and equipment and running Randolph's ship aground before abandoning it. It was a harbinger of a more consequential attack.

When James Randolph died in December 1781, his brother took over his businesses and the saltworks. Daniel Randolph lobbied for New Jersey State Troops to protect Toms River. In January, a former privateering partner of James drew the assignment. Joshua Huddy was put in command of two dozen men stationed in a blockhouse at the top of a hill overlooking the river. Daniel Randolph would join them.

DEFENDING TOMS RIVER

The ramshackle fort was more a rough stockade than an impregnable blockhouse. It overlooked a bridge and a storehouse. Twenty-five men lived within the unfinished palisades of upright timbers, six or seven feet high, sharpened at the tops. Four corner swivel guns, probably repurposed from a privateer, were the heaviest armaments. Loopholes were cut every few timbers to give the defenders firing holes for their muskets.

Since there was no gate or roof on the fort, Huddy's troops used portable ladders to get in and out. They spent their days fixing the walls, standing guard duty and cooking meals in the fireplace of the rude cabin and bunkhouse. They prepared, more or less, for an attack they thought would never come.

After seven long years of fighting, Huddy and his men were waiting out the winter and the war. The British had surrendered at Yorktown in Virginia three months earlier, making the small militia redoubt at Toms River an unlikely target. When an attack did come, its consequences went far beyond the Jersey Coast, thrusting the blockhouse commander into international renown.

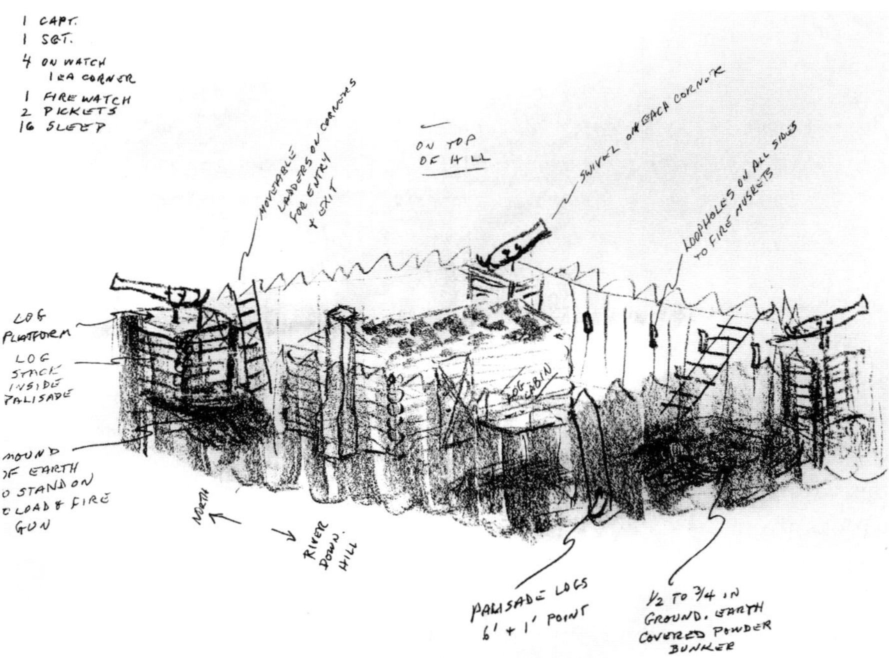

Opposite: Sketch of the Toms River Blockhouse. *Collection of the Ocean County Historical Society.*

Right: A typical swivel gun. *Public domain.*

Dillon's Island (today's Island Heights), between Toms River and James Randolph's plantation, was home to Loyalist William Dillon. A Freehold court had once convicted him of spying for the Associated Loyalists.

Dillon was under a sentence of death when he escaped from prison. He began trading contraband up and down the coast. His sloop *Lucy* was seized in March 1782. It was taken to Toms River while a Prize Court decided how to distribute its cargo, as noted by Judge Abiel Akin:

> *Notice is hereby given, That a Court will be held at the house of James Green, at Freehold, in the county of Monmouth, on the 16th day of March next, at the hour of ten o'clock of the forenoon of the same day, then and there to try the truth of the facts alleged in the bill of Captain William Gray (who as well, &c.,) against the sloop or vessel called the "Lucy," taken on her voyage from Egg Harbor to New York, William Dillon late master, with her tackle, furniture and cargo, and a negro man named York. To the end and intent that the owner or owners of said vessel, or any other person or persons interested therein, may appear and show cause, if any they have, why the said cargo and negro man should not be condemned to the captors pursuant to the prayer of said bill.*

BRITISH RESPONSE

Above: William Franklin. *New York Public Library.*

Opposite: The Blockhouse Battle. *Monmouth County Historical Association.*

Dillon appealed to William Franklin for help in recovering his ship. Franklin recognized that a retaliatory strike to recover Dillon's vessel could also deliver a one-two punch to the rebels, destroying the blockhouse and the saltworks. He ordered 120 Refugees, Bucks County (Pennsylvania) Volunteers and armed British sailors to head for Toms River.

Under the command of a Lieutenant Blanchard, the squadron left New York City in whaleboats. From Sandy Hook, the armed brig HMS *Arrogant* escorted them south. Navigating Cranberry Inlet at high tide, the war party landed on Coates Point at the mouth of the Toms River. Around midnight on Saturday, March 23, they hooked up with local Pine-Robbers led by the vicious Richard Davenport. Early the next morning, William Dillon guided the expedition to the blockhouse.

A saltworks lookout named Garret Irons saw the invaders. He ran the seven miles to the blockhouse to warn the militia. Joshua Huddy sent out a small scouting group to reconnoiter. Several were killed along a shore road by the Refugees. A larger British force had split off, hiking through the woods so they could approach the blockhouse from the north. They took James Johnson hostage before he could alert Huddy.

At daybreak, Lieutenant Blanchard's troops were hiding just outside the fort, behind a barn owned by Jacob Applegate. He and his son Bart were constrained to prevent them from crying out. Blanchard got as near to the fort as he dare, demanding its surrender. Huddy defiantly shouted back, "Come and take it!" The British obliged him, attacking with a fusillade of fire, killing John Farr. They threw up improvised ladders to scale the sharpened log walls.

The defenders lost half a dozen men during the first assault but successfully repelled it with musket fire, bayonets and long pikes. Two British officers died, and five enlisted men were wounded. A second attempt to get over the ramparts fared no better. When the Brits finally got inside, the close combat

"Come and take it!" —

ATTACK BY THE BRITISH ON THE BLOCK HOUSE AT TOM'S RIVER, 1782.

was brutal. Moses Robbins took a musket ball to his face. John Wainwright was hit with six bullets before succumbing. James Kinsley was shot in the head. Two others died in hand-to-hand fighting. Loyalist Lieutenant Inslee was killed, provoking his enraged companions to bayonet the captive James Johnson. He somehow survived.

Huddy was a whirling dervish during the intense battle. He sprinted from one wall to another, firing as he ran at anyone who made it to the top, forcing some back with his bayonet. He carried wounded men inside the cabin. He hustled ammunition to his troops, exhorting them to keep fighting. Despite the noise, smoke and musket balls, Huddy didn't get a scratch. Daniel Randolph said that Huddy did "all that a brave man could do to defend himself against so superior a number."

With powder and ammunition running perilously low, Huddy knew that his outnumbered men could no longer withstand full-on attacks. As wave after wave of Loyalists jumped inside the palisades, Huddy surrendered to save those still standing. John Cook refused to give up and was bayonetted to death by an unnamed Black man. Eight militiamen escaped in the confusion.

Nine militiamen were dead and several wounded. Huddy, nine of his surviving men and seven civilians were taken prisoner. The Loyalists lost Lieutenants Iredell and Inslee and a Black Refugee (name unknown); six were wounded. The whole bloody thing took less than fifteen minutes.

The victors burned the blockhouse down, spiked the four swivel cannons and threw them into the river. They torched a dozen homes "in which none but a piratical set of banditti resided." William Dillon pointed out which of his former neighbors' dwellings should be destroyed. At the top of his list were the house and tavern of Abiel Akin, the justice of the peace who'd advertised the sale of *Lucy*. Dillon made sure that the house of the wounded militiaman and brother-in-law of the Randolphs, Moses Robbins, went up in flames. Jacob Applegate, a nephew of Huddy's wife, Catherine, watched his home and barn turn to ashes. Of the two homes spared, one belonged to Dillon's niece.

Bart Applegate and his brother-in-law Garret Irons were released, set adrift in a small boat without oars or sails. Paddling through the bay with their bare hands and floorboards improvised for oars, the pair eventually made it back to shore.

Blanchard's troops destroyed gristmills and sawmills, storehouses and the saltworks. If *Lucy* was still anchored in the river at the time of the battle, its recovery wasn't reported. Nonetheless, Dillon had his revenge.

The blockhouse POWs were thrown into the *Arrogant*'s holds. When it docked in New York on March 25, Joshua Huddy, Daniel Randolph and Jacob Fleming were thrown into the old Sugar House prison.

A chronicler brought the consequential event into stark focus:

> *Toms River had been baptized in flame, bathed in blood, devoted to destruction. She had undergone the ordeal of fire. Her defenders had been killed or captured. Her houses, stores, barns, mills, and shops had been given over to the flames. Her most prominent and useful citizens had been carried away to British prison-ships. She lay prostrate in her ruin.*

Joshua Huddy's ruin was not far off.

Chapter 15

THE ROAD TO GRAVELLY POINT

His death excited the greatest indignation throughout the country.
—Benson J. Lossing

Hundreds of Americans rotted inside the walls of the dank New York prison. The Old Sugar House was anything but sweet for POWs during the Revolutionary War. Under ghastly conditions of filth and starvation, men died to the indifference, if not the delight, of their jailers. Despite the war's denouement, the British were happy to message that no rebel was beyond their reach—malefactors like Joshua Huddy would be severely punished.

Though hardened by years of conflict, few men survived extended confinement in the infamous prison. Joshua Huddy, as tough as they come, might have made it, but he wasn't kept in the death trap for long.

Confined in New York

The Toms River prisoners, Huddy, Daniel Randolph and Jacob Fleming stayed in the Sugar House for a week. On April 1, they were moved to the Provost Jail, only marginally colder than its warden, Captain William Cunningham, "the like of whom, for unpitying, relentless cruelty, the world has not produced, thirsted for blood, and took an eager delight in murder."

While the blockhouse rebels languished in the Provo, a once-captured Refugee Samuel Taylor met with former New Jersey governor William Franklin of the Associated Loyalists. Taylor sought orders to hang Huddy for murdering Philip White and Daniel Randolph for the presumed death of Clayton Tilton.

Opposite: Joshua Huddy was moved from the Sugar House prison. *Public domain.*

Right: Joshua Huddy's second confinement was at New York's Provost Jail. *Public domain.*

Franklin agreed to "give the necessary orders if [Taylor] thought he would execute Huddy." Taylor enthused, "He need not fear that." When Taylor was reassigned to a different mission, Richard Lippincott got the call. The Loyalist captain was even more hell-bent on retribution—Philip White was his cousin.

Lippincott's Griefs and Grievances

Richard Lippincott had a long series of personal losses and wartime insults. His first wife died within a year of their marriage. He and his second wife buried two young daughters.

He was a partner at a Manasquan saltworks with his brother-in-law Jeremiah Borden and William Corlies and briefly a militiaman before switching allegiance. Late in 1776, Lippincott was taken prisoner, caught with copies of General Sir William Howe's pardon for rebels pledging loyalty to King George III. Lippincott escaped the Burlington Gaol and joined the British army in New York.

In June 1779, Lippincott conducted a surprise attack in Shrewsbury. A dozen Continental troops were quartered at the Sign of the Blue Ball Tavern just opposite Christ Church at the town's prominent intersection. The bored

Above: The Blue Ball Tavern (*far left*) was catty-corner to Christ Church, Shrewsbury. *Monmouth County Historical Association.*

Left: The damaged orb is preserved at Christ Church. *Rick Geffken.*

American guards had amused themselves by taking target practice at a crown on Christ Church's steeple. The crown, atop a weather vane with an orb, represented England's domination of its colonies. Maybe their aim was off or they shot at an easier target, but their musket balls hit the orb.

Bound for punishing this affront to their fealty and religion, Richard Lippincott and four other Refugees left Sandy Hook and rowed up Parkers Creek toward Shrewsbury. They hid behind Christ Church gravestones, watching the Continentals relax outside the tavern without any sentries posted. The Refugees charged across the dirt road and burst into the tavern, grabbing muskets left unattended in a corner and smashing the weapons against a tree. They bayonetted three soldiers to death and took nine prisoners back to Sandy Hook during what came to be known as the Allen House Massacre.

Huddy to Sandy Hook

In the early morning hours of April 8, 1782, Lippincott with John and Ezekiel Tilton abruptly roused Huddy, who was still shackled hand and feet in irons. The Tilton brothers had assumed that General Forman's declaration that their brother "Clate Tilton shall be hanged!" was fait accompli. They craved justice.

If the militia captain figured that he was about to be exchanged for a British officer, he was dead wrong. A Provo jailer contemptuously suggested that if Huddy had known what was really intended "he would not go out so joyfully as he did." Huddy, Daniel Randolph and Jacob Fleming were escorted to a sloop waiting in the East River. The three captives were hoisted aboard a ship in Sandy Hook's Spermaceti Cove the next day. The HMS *Britannia* was under the command of Captain Richard Morris.

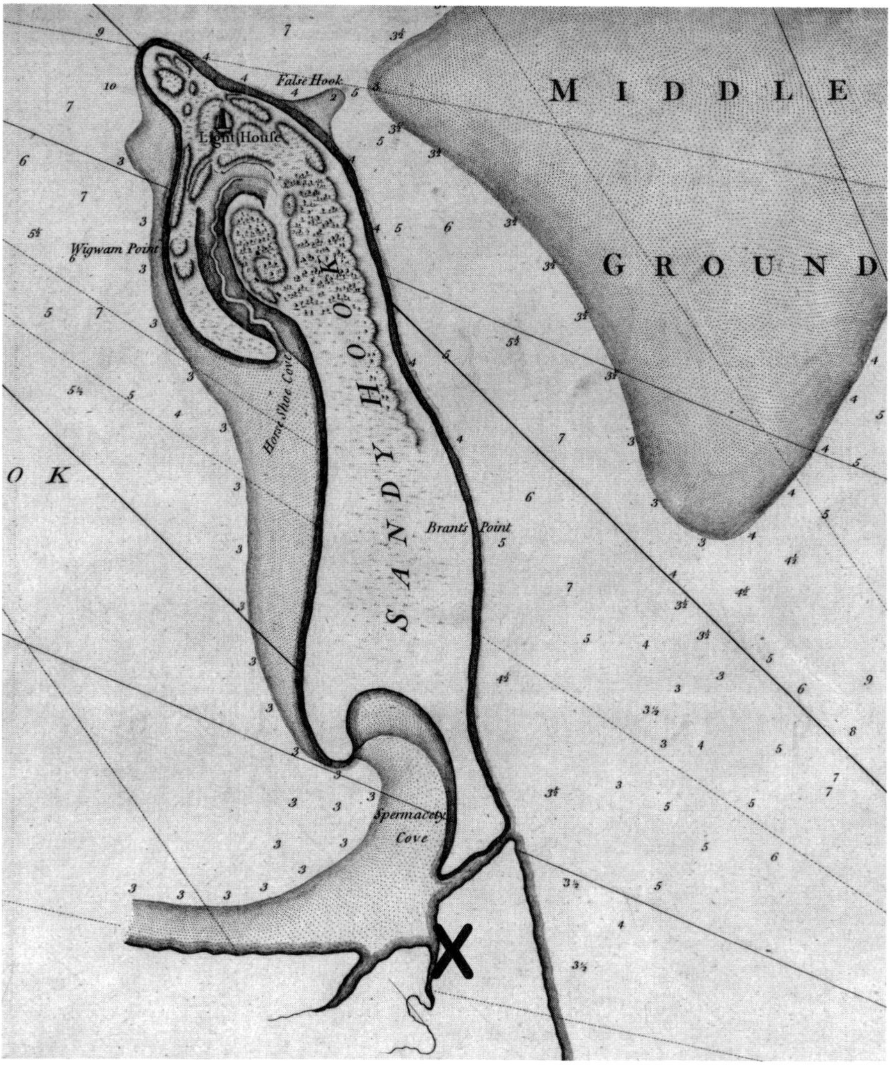

Opposite: Richard Lippincott leaving the brig *Britannia* with Joshua Huddy. *©2023 Steve Schreiber/Monmouth Timeline.*

Above: Gravelly Point (X) in Highlands below Spermaceti Cove. *Library of Congress.*

If Richard Lippincott needed another rationale for what he was planning, he got a strong one. William Cunningham told him that Huddy had confessed to the 1778 hanging of Stephen Edwards, "a worthy loyalist, and the first of our brethren who fell a martyr to Republican fury in Monmouth County." The provost marshal quoted Huddy admitting that he "ty'd the knot and slushed [greased] the rope well, and that Col. Forman assisted in pulling the rope hand over hand." This was either a Cunningham lie or the hyperbolic words of a defiant prisoner to the detested jailer. Regardless, it more than enough for Lippincott.

Lippincott knew dammed well that Huddy hadn't killed Philip White. As Huddy himself pointed out, "It was impossible I could have taken Philip White, I being a prisoner in New York, closely confined, and for many days before he [White] was made a prisoner." The Loyalist captain rejected the denial out of hand.

To Richard Morris's question about what he was going to do with Huddy, Lippincott answered that he would "put the orders he had received from the Refugee Board in execution which was to hang him." His written orders were clearly different:

> *To Mr. Commissary Challoner. New York, April 8th, 1782*
>
> *Sir—Deliver to Capt. Richard Lippincott the three following persons: Lieutenant Joshua Huddy, Daniel Rudolph, and Jacob Fleming, to take down to the Hook, to procure the exchange of Capt. Clayton Tilton and two other Associated Royalists.*
>
> *By order of the Board of Directors of Associated Loyalist.*
> *S.S. Blowers, Secretary.*

On board the *Britannia*, Lippincott waved some papers at Richard Morris. The brig's captain saw one was already signed, obviously written earlier at the Associated Loyalists offices. Its last ominous line read, "Up goes Huddy for White."

Gravelly Point

On April 12, Lippincott, John Tilton and several Refugees lowered the *Britannia*'s ships boat. Huddy's hands were tied behind him as the detail rowed to the Highlands hills across the bay, headed for a creek below Esek Hartshorne's house. Lippincott had picked the spot on purpose. He could have executed Huddy on Sandy Hook, but Gravelly Point was a nasty reminder of the Monmouth Militia's defeat on that very hillside five years before.

The boat's bow scratched into the sand and mud a few yards into the creek. The men pulled up their oars and hopped out, splashing into the shallows. Trudging through the muck and complaining as only soldiers can, the Refugees kicked aside seaweed and horseshoe crabs trapped in shallow tidal pools. The place smelled of decay and death. The marshy wetlands sucked at their boots as they headed for a path leading down from the hills. They needed solid ground and a tall tree.

The Refugees threw a rope over "a limb of an old bass-wood tree." Huddy dictated his will to one of the Refugees, who wrote it on the top of a barrel rolled from the boat. For years afterward, a Middletown school master boasted that he was the man who wrote it on a piece of foolscap paper. The unnamed man claimed that his part in the hanging was justified since "in war times men could do many things that they could not do in times of peace." Whether or not he was actually there, he understood human nature well enough.

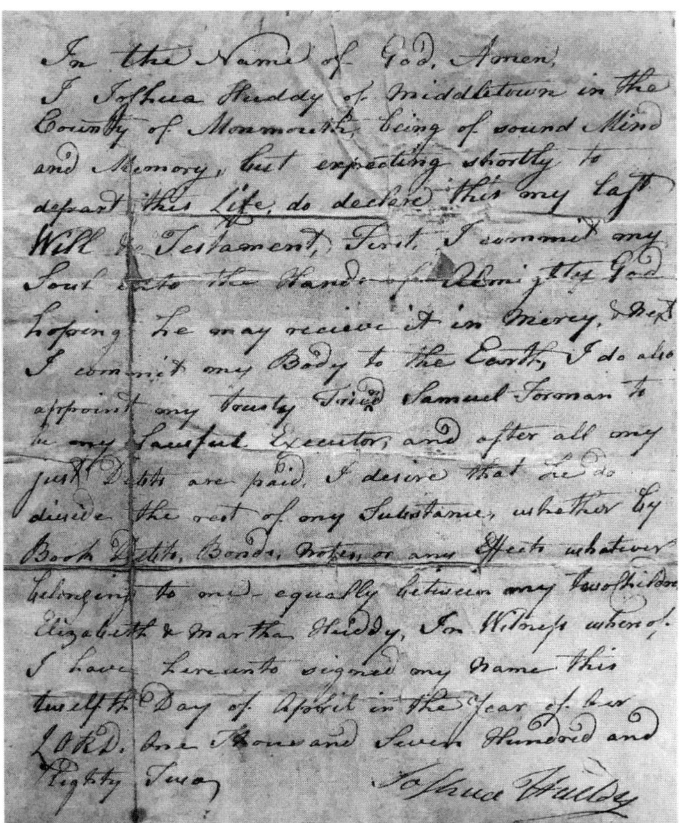

In the Name of God, Amen;
I Joshua Huddy of Middletown in the County of Monmouth, being of sound Mind and Memory, but expecting shortly to depart this Life, do declare this my last Will & Testament, First, I commit my Soul into the Hands of Almighty God hoping he may receive it in mercy, & next I commit my Body to the Earth, I do also appoint my trusty Friend Samuel Forman to be my lawful Executor, and after all my just Debts are paid, I desire that he do divide the rest of my Substance, whether by Book Debts, Bonds, Notes or any Effects whatever belonging to me — equally between my two Children Elizabeth & Martha Huddy, In Witness whereof I have hereunto signed my Name this twelfth Day of April in the Year of our LORD, One Thousand Seven Hundred and Eighty Two

Joshua Huddy

Joshua Huddy's name on the second line of his will does not match his signature at the bottom, indicating that the text was written by someone else. *New Jersey Historical Society.*

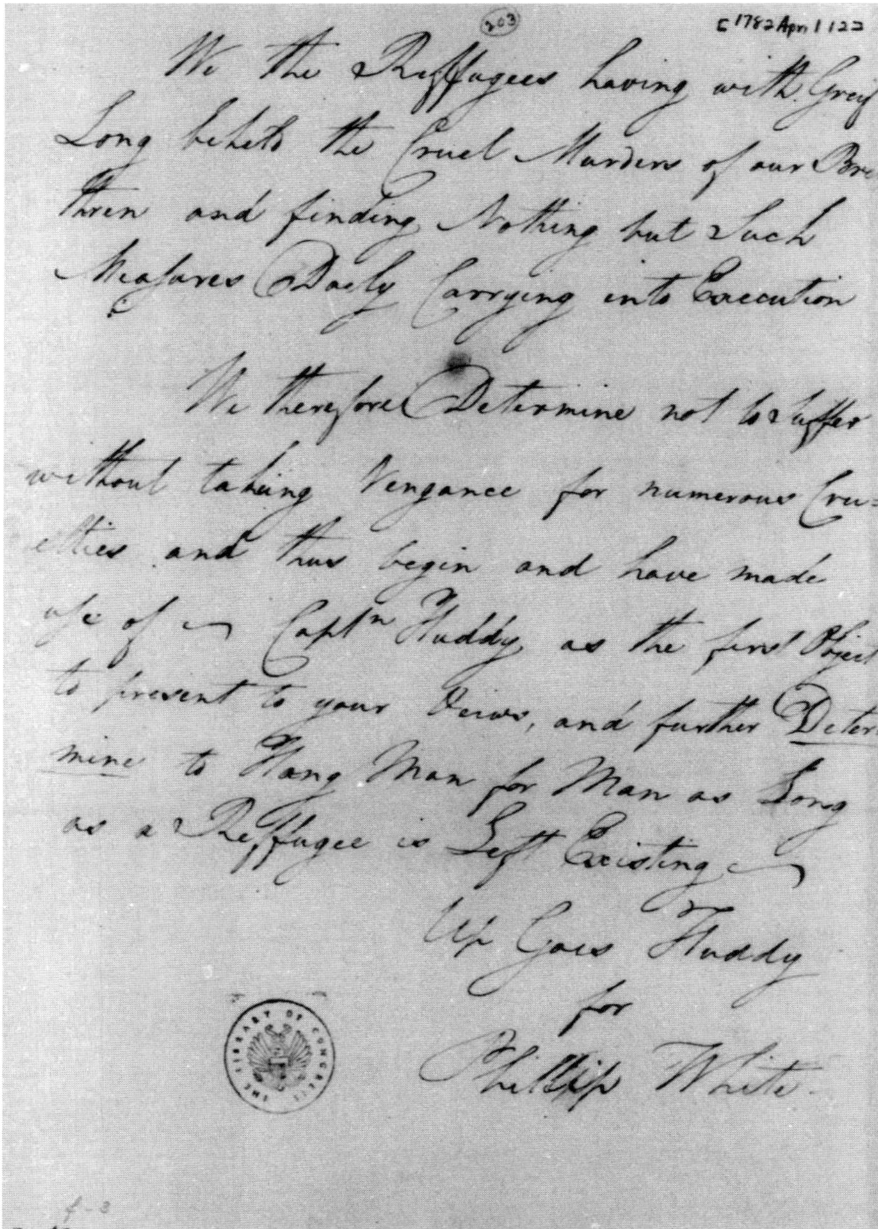

[1782 Apr 12]

We the Reffugees having with Grief Long beheld the Cruel Murders of our Brethren and finding Nothing but Such Measures Daily Carrying into Execution

We therefore Determine not to Suffer without taking Vengance for numerous Cruelties and thus begin and have made use of Captn Huddy as the first Object to present to your Views, and further Determine to Hang Man for Man as Long as a Reffugee is Left Existing.

Up Goes Huddy for Phillip White.

The note pinned on Huddy. *Library of Congress.*

At ten o'clock in the morning, Huddy was forced to stand on the barrel with a noose around his neck. He allegedly shook hands with Lippincott and said stoically, "I shall die innocent and in a good cause." Daniel Randolph said that Huddy exuded "uncommon composure of mind and fortitude [as he] prepared himself for his end."

Lippincott pinned the note Captain Morris had seen on Huddy's chest. Morris saw "a Negroe" knock the barrel out from under Huddy. His executioners smirked at his suffocating grunts and flailing kicks, shouting "Hurrah!" when his squirming ceased. In their disdain, they left Huddy's body dangling from the tree.

Returning to the boat, Lippincott must have smiled about having one fewer rebel bastard to worry about. John Tilton was impressed that Huddy "dyed with the firmness of a Lyon." (The embellishment that Refugees at Horseshoe Cove cheered when Huddy died can't be true. It was two miles distant, too far for anyone to witness Huddy's final agony.)

In the late afternoon, a widow living nearby reported grim news. Something was swinging back and forth on the beach. Friends came to cut down the limp body with the note still on the victim's jacket, his will inside a pocket. Huddy's body was covered reverently and gently laid in a wagon. Distraught and angry, they took Joshua Huddy on his last, long journey to Freehold. The small cortege shuttled along slowly, passing places of former heroics and Huddy's Colts Neck home and tavern. They stopped now and then so tearful mourners could touch the hero's pall while offering prayers and tributes.

The Survivors

Daniel Randolph and Jacob Fleming were subsequently exchanged for two men still very much alive in the Freehold Jail, Clayton Tilton and Aaron White. The latter's favorable testimony about who was actually responsible for Philip White's death came too late to save Joshua Huddy.

Brothers Ezekiel, John and Clayton Tilton joined the British army after their Middletown estates were confiscated in 1779. Loyalists to the core and united in their hatred of the rebels, the Tiltons met very different ends.

Some months after Huddy perished, Ezekiel Tilton was fishing in Sandy Hook Bay when rebels in an armed whaleboat captured him. He was brought to the Freehold Jail. His wife, Elizabeth, wrote to Sir Guy Carleton. Her husband was "loaded with irons" and "daily threatened with death." Couldn't the commander of the British army in New York do something? Refugees petitioned for Carleton to intervene before a "rebel commander will murder the man without some orders to the contrary from his superiors."

Carlton wrote to New Jersey Governor William Livingston in late July, "I hereby demand Sir, that this man shall be placed in the Condition of a prisoner of war only and treated with that lenity with which prisoners of war ought to be treated." Carleton warned the governor to be careful not to "violate laws of war or excite resentment in the Loyalists." Could Carleton not have seen his own hypocrisy?

Livingston maintained that Tilton was a traitor who had "been guilty of house-robbing, house-burning, horse stealing and plundering." Ezekiel Tilton was hanged on December 13, 1782. His brothers survived the war and immigrated to New Brunswick, Canada, where John died in 1805, apparently of natural causes. Clayton was killed in 1808 trying to round up Loyalist deserters.

Chapter 16

REPERCUSSIONS, FOREIGN AND DOMESTIC

Captain Huddy was not himself renowned.
The world's sympathy and interest were not in the man Huddy,
but in the events of vital importance clustered about his death.
—M.C. Murray Hyde

Word of Joshua Huddy's death spread like a Pinelands wildfire. New Jersey and New York papers were full of the dreadful news, seen here in the *Independent Gazetteer, or The Chronicle of Freedom*:

> *April 20, 1782. We hear from Monmouth, East New-Jersey, that Captain Huddy, one of the Prisoners taken at the Surrender of the Block-House, at Tom's River, on the 24th ult. Was a few Days ago brought over the Gut between Never-Sinks and Sandy-Hook, and privately hanged on Hartshorn's Plantation, near that Place, by a mixed Company of Negroes, Tories and Englishmen. A Paper was found affixed to this unhappy Man, assigning the Reasons for their Conduct. It is further added that the People of Monmouth were determined to retaliate, and a Captain Tilton, a Prisoner in Monmouth Jail, was fixed on for that Purpose.*

Angry citizens showed up at the Monmouth County Court House on April 14, 1782. They were just beginning to relax into a prewar normalcy when they were suddenly shocked back to reality. The four hundred distraught people on Main Street demanded an official response to the atrocity. Some called for the immediate hanging of the Loyalist Clayton Tilton.

The *New Jersey Gazette* did its part to rile up folks throughout New Jersey and New York:

> *Last Saturday was brought to this place the corpse of captain Joshua Huddy, who was, about ten o'clock the day before, most barbarously and unwarrantable hanged, at Middletown-Point, by a party of refugees. This murder was attended with so much deliberate injustice and wanton cruelty, that the circumstances ought to be preserved and made public, not only to call upon the vengeance of his countrymen to expiate the manes* [soul of the dead] *of the sufferer, but as a shocking instance of the blackness of that guilt of which human nature is capable.*

Huddy Taken to Freehold

Huddy's remains lay at the home of Captain James Green, captured by Colonel Tye in 1778. Green's house was where Abiel Akin's Prize Court met the week before to decide how to divvy up the claims on the sloop *Lucy*.

Reverend John T. Woodhull. *Public domain.*

Reverend John Tennent Woodhull rode over from his residence at the Old Parsonage. He was an ardent Patriot who'd spent almost two years as chaplain of the Fifth Lancaster (Pennsylvania) Battalion Militia. He was at the Battle at Monmouth when his Old Tennent Church served as a field hospital for Continental troops. Woodhull added sparks to the crowd's emotional kindling when he preached Joshua Huddy's funeral sermon on the Court House piazza adjacent to Green's.

Woodhull's ministry at Old Tennent suggests that Joshua Huddy's final resting place was in the church's graveyard, but its actual location is lost. One hundred years after Huddy died, historian William S. Stryker, believing that the hero deserved a grave site marker and decorations, wrote to the family. An elderly Huddy relative responded that "the precise burial place of Captain Huddy is unknown to us…the family always assumed it was at Old Tennent." Unfortunately, the church had no records confirming his burial. One reason may be the competing tradition that Huddy's remains were taken "to some burial ground near Colts Neck."

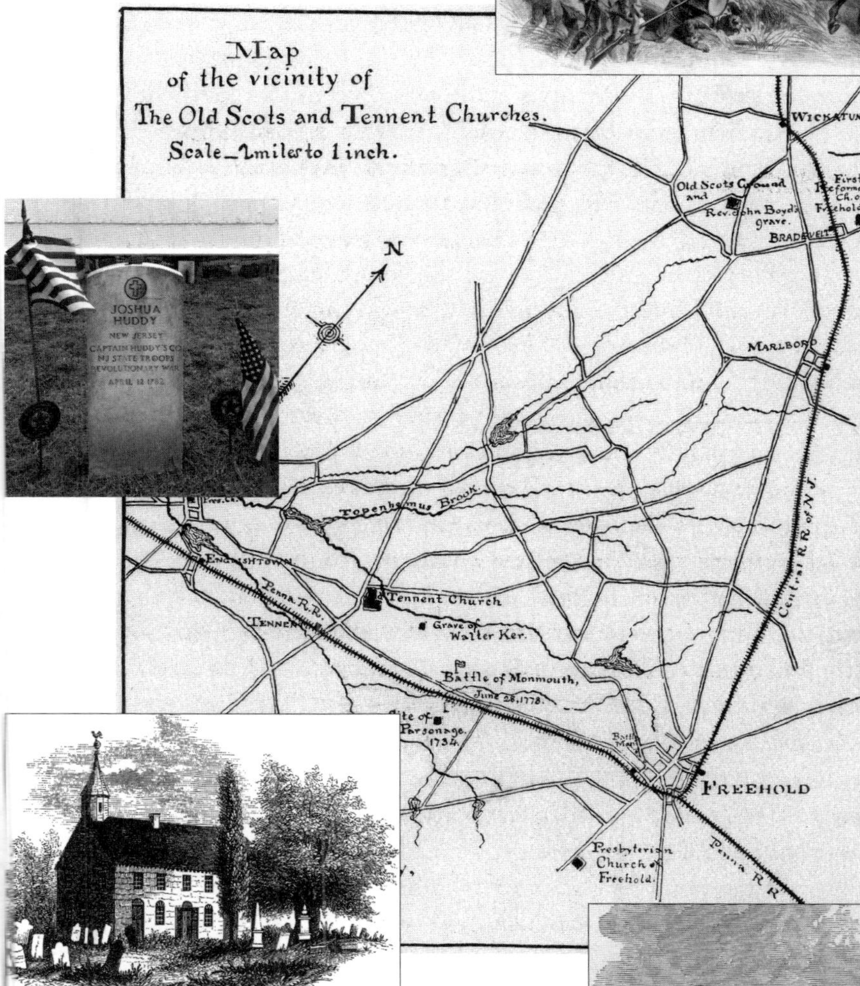

Map of the Vicinity of the Old Scots and Tennent Church. Monmouth County Historical Association.

Insets, clockwise from top left: Joshua Huddy's cenotaph at Old Tennent. *Rick Geffken*; George Washington at the Battle of Monmouth. *National Archives*; The Old Parsonage. *Public domain*; Old Tennent Church. *Public domain.*

At the conclusion of Huddy's funeral ceremony, an agitated Reverend Woodhull confronted David Forman. Woodhull demanded, "We must retaliate, or the Tories will overpower us."

Forman agreed. "Yes, we will hang every Tory we can get hold of." The unmollified Woodhull kept pushing. "The British care not how many Tories we hang—they do not feel the loss. But we must retaliate on a British officer of the same rank with Huddy, among the prisoners of war, and hang him. That will make them feel, and make them more cautious how they commit such acts of violence." The wheels of justice, and revenge, began turning.

Demands for Retaliation

Responding to public outrage, Monmouth Militia and political leaders immediately drafted a petition to George Washington demanding accountability for Huddy's murder:

> *The inhabitants of the county of Monmouth being assembled on account of the horrid and almost unparalleled murder of Captain Joshua Huddy, by the Refugees from New York, and as we presume by the approbation, if not by the express command, of the British Commander in Chief, Sir Henry Clinton, hold it as our indispensable duty, as well to the United States in general, as ourselves in particular, to shew to Your Excellency, that the aforesaid Captain Joshua Huddy, late commanding the Post at Toms-river, was after a very brave and gallant defence made a prisoner of war…on Friday the twelfth instant, a party of Refugees, said to have been commanded by a Captain Richard Lippincott, brought the said Captain Huddy over to the High-Lands of Middletown, and hanged him.…And We do with the fullest assurance, rely upon receiving effectual support from Your Excellency…as the Person in whom the sole power of avenging our wrongs is lodged, and who has full and ample authority, to bring a British officer of the same rank to a similar end.*
>
> *Samuel Forman*
> *Peter Forman*
> *Barns Smock*
> *Asher Holmes*
> *John Smock*
> *John Covenhoven*
> *Richd Cox*
> *John Schanck*
> *Elisha Walton*
> *Thomas Chadwick*
> *Thos Seabrook*
> *Joseph Stillwell*
> *Wm Willcocks*
> *Stephen Fleming*

Washington sent a sharply worded letter to his British counterpart, Henry Clinton, as reported in the *Pennsylvania Packet*:

> *Head-Quarters, April 21, 1782. Sir, The inclosed representation, from the Inhabitants of the County of Monmouth, with testimonials to the fact (which can be corroborated by other unquestionable evidence) will bring before your Excellency the most wanton, cruel, and unprecedented murder that ever disgraced the arms of a civilized people.... Candor obliges me to be explicit.... I demand the guilty—Captain Lippincott, therefore or the officer who commanded at the execution of Captain Huddy must be given up; or, if that Officer was of inferior rank to him, so many of the perpetrators, as will, according to the Tariff of Exchange be an Equivalent.*

Clinton's reply showed understanding and annoyance: "[T]hough I am extremely concerned for the cause, I cannot conceal my surprise and displeasure at the very improper language you made use of." He admitted that he knew about Huddy's death and had already ordered "a strict inquiry" to "bring the perpetrators of it to an immediate trial."

That inquiry resulted in an April 27 letter from the Board of Loyalists President William Franklin to Clinton. In a classic example of plausible deniability, William Franklin responded to General Sir Henry Clinton, contending that he didn't authorize Huddy's execution but that it was nonetheless justified:

> *Three prisoners delivered to Captain Lippencot* [sic] *on the 8th instant, were not exchanged according to the intention of the Board, but they were nevertheless disposed of in a manner which the Board are clearly of opinion was highly justifiable from the general principles of necessity, and the peculiar nature and circumstances of the case.... Randolph and Fleming were both exchanged for Captain* [Clayton] *Tilton. Captain Lippencot, on his first return from Sandy Hook, made a report, in writing, of the 18 oar barge... and mentioned verbally to one or two members* [of the Board], *that Huddy was exchanged* [emphasizing the word] *for Philip White.... With regard to the circumstances respecting the reported death of Joshua Huddy, they* [the Board] *know nothing.*

Franklin went on to contradict himself:

> *The many daring acts of the same nature which have been perpetrated with impunity, by a set of vindictive Rebels, well known by the name of Monmouth Retaliators, associated and headed by one General Furman* [Forman], *whose horrid acts of cruelty have gained him universally the name of Black David.... We thought it high time to convince the rebels, we would no longer tamely submit to such glaring acts of barbarity.... We therefore pitched upon Joshua Huddy for a proper subject for retaliation, because he was not only well known to have been a very active and cruel persecutor of our friends, but had not been ashamed to boast of his having been instrumental in hanging Stephen Edwards.*

Franklin was convinced that retaliatory executions of rebels had "the desired effect" of reducing violence against Loyalists. He excused Lippincott's actions and, remarkably, asserted that Loyalists only committed heinous crimes to stop the heinous crimes of the rebels.

Clinton used Franklin's allegations to reject Washington's request to turn Lippincott in for punishment: "To sacrifice Innocence under the Notion of preventing Guilt, in Place of suppressing, would be adopting brutality and raising it to the greatest height."

His public stance aside, Clinton was hemmed in by his unpopularity with the Tories. He believed that the unruly Refugees were an impediment to peace. At the same time, he knew that giving up a Refugee officer would risk provoking an even more intense rivalry with the independent Associated Loyalists. Clinton decided to stall.

Washington and Clinton were deeply traditional military leaders. On May 2, 1782, Clinton, hoping that a compromise would calm the contentious issue, appointed Major General James Paterson as president of a general court-martial for "the misbehaviour of any Officer, Soldier, or any other person under my Command."

Washington responded in kind, asking New Jersey's Governor William Livingston to inform "all persons acting in a military capacity in your State" that they would be punished for violations to the laws of war or turned over to the British.

Clinton's command position had been in jeopardy since the Yorktown surrender. He was recalled to England on May 6 and replaced by Sir Guy Carleton. Carleton believed that Huddy's murder violated the traditions of military justice. He assured Washington "that he desired to pursue every

Thomas Paine. *Library of Congress.*

measure that might tend to prevent these criminal excesses in individuals."

Pressure ratcheted up. In an open letter to Sir Guy Carleton, the political philosopher Thomas Paine expressed outrage. The English-born Paine ridiculed his former countrymen: "What sort of men must Englishmen be…when under the eye and nose of their commander in chief, a prisoner [Huddy] can be taken at pleasure at his confinement, and his death made a matter of sport?…the murderer [Lippincott] is within your lines."

If Carleton hadn't realized the seriousness of the situation before, Paine's impassioned letter put him on high alert. Managing this chapter of what Paine had long called "The Crisis" would take time and diplomacy on both sides.

British Court-Martial

Richard Lippincott's military trial convened in New York on May 3, 1782. General Paterson and fourteen other high-ranking British officers considered the charge:

> *Captain Richard Lippincott, of the aforesaid Loyalists, was brought Prisoner before the Court, accused of the Murder of Joshua Huddy, a Prisoner of War to the Associated Loyalists, by hanging, or causing him to be hanged by the Neck until he was dead. He having received said Huddy into his Custody, for the purpose of Exchanging him for another Prisoner of War by Virtue of an Order from the Honorable Board of Directors of Associated Loyalists dated April 8th 1782.*

In his opening statements, Lippincott played the victim, a bystander to the whims of others. He claimed that the court had no authority over him because he was "not an enlisted Soldier, nor paid nor Mustered as a Soldier, nor is he an Officer in pay and with Rank, and therefore he saith, that he is not liable by any Court Martial for the said supposed Crime." He claimed that he was "legally held to Answer for the said supposed offence, before a Court of Common Law cognizance, and not elsewhere." The court disagreed, prompting Lippincott to plead not guilty.

Witnesses for the prosecution included John and Ezekiel Tilton, Richard Morris of the *Britannia*, Captain William Cunningham, officials from the Board of Directors of the Associated Loyalists and Sandy Hook Refugees. Defense witnesses said that Lippincott had proposed an expedition to the Freehold Jail to free Clayton Tilton. Others reiterated how the rebels murdered their Loyalist colleagues.

Lippincott was adamant that he had replied positively when Franklin asked, "Will you execute him [Huddy] when you take him out?" Franklin nodded, saying, "Then you shall have him." John Tilton said he heard it too.

Lippincott maintained that he hadn't acted out of personal malice, only that Huddy's "life was taken for the recent Murder of Philip White, to effect the public end of humanity by preventing a repetition of the like barbarities."

The defendant's most powerful testimony was his assertion that his

> *whole conduct was open and undisguised. I waited upon Governor Franklin at his own desire, to receive his orders. I took them with the most unsuspicious Confidence that he spoke the Language of the Board & had power to command one. I affected no Secrecy. I carried the Label for Huddy* [the note affixed to Huddy's breast during the hanging] *to the Board Room. It was notorious to Many before we left New York. I disclosed my Orders to Capt. Morris of the Guard Ship. Every man of my Party…was confident that we had Governor Franklin's Orders & if I had not had them I must have been the greatest idiot in Nature to Act as I then did.*

On Saturday, June 22, two months after Joshua Huddy was killed, the president of the court, General Paterson, declared:

> *The Court having considered the Evidence for and against the Prisoner, Captain Richard Lippincott, together with what he had to offer in his Defence, and it appearing that (altho' Joshua Huddy was executed without proper Authority) What the Prisoner did in the Matter was not the Effect of Malice or Ill-will, but proceeded from a Conviction that it was his Duty to obey the Orders of the Board of Directors of Associated Loyalists, and his not doubting their having a full Authority to give such Orders, the Court is of Opinion that he, the Prisoner, Captain Richard Lippincott, is Not Guilty of the Murder laid to his Charge, and doth therefore Acquit him.*

With Lippincott's exoneration, the court, in effect, found William Franklin responsible for Huddy's execution. Shortly after the verdict was announced, militia Captain Adam Huyler led an indignant group of Huddy's friends to New York to try to kidnap Richard Lippincott at his residence. The attempt to administer their own sweet revenge failed, as Lippincott wasn't home when they got there.

Carleton delayed sending the transcript of Lippincott's trial to George Washington until the end of July. He wrote to Washington that "notwithstanding the acquittal of Lippincott, he reprobated the measure, and gave assurances of prosecuting a farther enquiry." To demonstrate his sincerity, Carleton revoked the military powers of the Board of Associated Loyalists.

In August, William Franklin left for England. The rift between him and his father, Benjamin, was the most famous family division of the Revolutionary War. William he lived in exile until his 1813 death in London. The Franklins never reconciled.

George Washington's Impatience

During the month-and-a-half-long Lippincott trial, George Washington developed a contingency plan. On the day Lippincott's trial began in New York, he instructed Brigadier General Moses Hazen to "immediately on receipt of this, designate, by Lot for the above purpose, a British Captain who is an unconditional Prisoner, if such a one is in your possession; if not, a Lieutenant under the same circumstances from among the Prisoners at any of the Posts either in Pennsylvania or Maryland."

Hazen was at York, Pennsylvania, guarding the British prisoners of war taken at Yorktown in Virginia. The POWs were on parole, allowing them limited movement. Hazen hesitated to obey Washington's order because the men were not "unconditionals," just the opposite—the terms of the Yorktown capitulation agreement said they could not be punished. Washington wrote again a few weeks later, insisting that a British captain be selected regardless of status.

Still uncomfortable with Washington's orders, Hazen met with the most senior British POW, Major James Gordon, to assemble thirteen of his fellow captives at Lancaster. Addressing the group with heartfelt empathy, Gordon announced, "Gentlemen, you will scarcely believe that in the face

Above: Captain Asgill (*dark hair*) seated below a Dragoon officer (*standing with helmet*) at the Black Bear Tavern. *Alan Birch/Creative Commons Attribution-Share Alike 4.0.*

Right: Captain Charles Asgill. *Library of Congress.*

of capitulation, and in defiance of strong remonstrances which I felt it my duty to make, both to the American and French authorities, one of you is doomed to suffer....I wish to God they would take me in your place." Gordon was in tears.

At the Black Bear Tavern on the following morning, May 26, Hazen read Washington's orders to the thirteen officers. He once again spoke of his personal regrets while asking them to pick one of their own. They refused, so Hazen decided on a lottery. Thirteen slips of paper with each officer's name were placed in a hat. A second hat held twelve blank papers and one labeled "Unfortunate." Two young American drummer boys were assigned to pick from each hat alternately.

Officer after officer exhaled as they drew blank slips. When his name was chosen for the fatal ballot, a captain sighed, "I knew how it would be, I never won so much as a bet of back-gammon, in my life."

On May 27, Hazen informed Washington that "the drawing of lots, which was done in the Presence of Major Gordon and all the British Captains within the Limits prescribed; the unfortunate Lot has fallen on the Honourable Capt. Charles Asgill, of the Guards; a young Gentleman of seventeen Years of Age." Hazen added:

> *I judge no Inconveniency can possibly arise to us by sending on Capt. Asgill, to Philadelphia, which will naturally tend to keep up the Hue and Cry, and of course foment the present Dissentions amongst our Enemies, I have sent him under guard as directed. Those Officers above-mentioned are not only of the Description which your Excellency wishes, and at first ordered, but in another Point of View are proper Subjects for Example, been Traitors to America, and having taken refuge with the Enemy, and by us in Arms. It have fallen to my Lot to superintend this melancholy disagreeable Duty, I must confess I have been most sensible affected with it, and* [do] *most sincerely wish that the Information here given may operate in favour of Youth, Innocence, and Honour.*

Neither Washington nor Hazen understood just how loud and far-reaching the "Hue and Cry" would become.

Asgill's Lot

Charles Asgill was born in 1763, the only son of Sir Charles Asgill, 1st Baronet, and Dame Sarah Theresa Pratviel, a wealthy French Huguenot émigré. The Baronet was a banker, a sheriff of the city of London and eventually Lord Mayor. Captain Charles Asgill was an officer in the Brigade of Guards when General Charles Cornwallis surrendered at Yorktown. The teenaged Asgill had been in America for only four months.

Major Gordon and a detail of Dragoons escorted Asgill from Lancaster to Philadelphia. For two days, he searched for ways to get the young officer out of his awful predicament. Gordon wrote to everyone of influence he could think of: Washington, Congress and the secretary of war. He sought out the French minister to the Americas for intervention. Asgill himself penned a note to Washington reiterating his protected status, adding, "nor do I know why my life should be an Atonement for the Misdemeanours [*sic*] of others." None of these pleadings yielded relief for Asgill.

On June 7, they arrived at Chatham, New Jersey. Continental Army Colonel Elias Dayton put them up in his home, letting the two British officers come and go as they pleased. When Washington heard about these loose arrangements, he wrote Dayton that Asgill must "be kept close prisoner, in perfect Security." Pending the outcome of Lippincott's trial in

Timothy Day's Chatham Tavern. *Wikimedia Commons.*

New York, Washington couldn't chance something happening to Asgill or, worse, his escape. Asgill was moved to Timothy Day's Tavern and confined to a small room.

With Asgill placed on a starvation diet of bread and water, his hope and vitality started to fade. Gordon raised some money for better food. Just for fun, local rebels started to harass the prisoner. For several nights, drunken rowdies bribed their way into Asgill's quarters, kept him awake for hours and once beat him severely. Washington changed his mind again, granting Asgill limited parole.

Major Gordon continued to reach out for a solution, even writing to Joshua Huddy's widow, Catherine. We don't know her feelings about the matter, but even if she agreed that Asgill shouldn't be executed, there was nothing she could do.

International Uproar

Naturally, the reactions to the Huddy-Lippincott-Asgill controversy differed on the opposite sides of the Atlantic world. The English public were ignorant of or chose to ignore the basic facts of Huddy's murder. They were easily swayed by emotional pleas justifying revenge, such as this July 1782 letter in the *London Chronicle* signed by "A Loyalist":

> *Finding in several papers a very partial and imperfect account of the motives which led to the execution of Captain Huddy, a rebel officer, I request you will publish the following facts and observations relative to that transaction…the principal rebels…have called in to their aid our most dangerous enemy* [France]…. [Our government used] *lenity in carrying on the war against its treacherous subjects, while in actual arms to destroy it.* [Any atrocities were] *the conduct of the Rebel States toward British subjects who have refused to unite in the usurpation, and have supported the cause of their Sovereign….And therefore when acts of cruelty, contrary to the laws of nations, are introduced on one side, a neglect on the other to retaliate is impolitic, inhuman, and criminal.* [When British Generals did retaliate] *rebel murders and assassinations immediately ceased, and the Loyalists, when taken, were treated with humanity and exchanged.*

King George III of England. *Library of Congress.*

A paroled British officer, who had also been captured at Yorktown, traveled to Baronet Asgill's London home to convey the plight of his son. Lord Charles was in such deteriorating health that a distraught Lady Sarah kept the news from her husband. She appealed for George III to intervene. The British monarch's nonchalant response was that "the execution of an officer under the circumstances of Captain Asgill must destroy all future confidence in Treatys & Capitulations." The king was indifferent to the trivialities of war, believing that Sir Guy Carleton would deal with the situation appropriately.

Lady Asgill was not satisfied with the British king's diplomatic vagueness. She sent a desperate letter to Charles Gravier, comte de Vergennes, the minister of foreign affairs to Louis XVI of France. Writing in her native French, she begged the seasoned diplomat to rescue her son. It was a brilliant gamble, given that England and France were still at war. Lady Asgill also knew that France was America's strongest European supporter. Dame Asgill filled her note with the passion only a mother could feel:

> *From Lady Asgill, 18 July 1782*
> *If the politeness of the French Court will permit an Application of a stranger....My son (an only son) and dear as he is brave, amiable as deserving to be so, only nineteen, a prisoner under the Articles of Capitulation of Yorktown, is now confined in America an object of retaliation! Shall the innocent suffer for the guilty?...surrounded as I am by objects of distress; distracted with fear and guilt...my husband given over by his physicians... and not in a state to be informed of the misfortune—my daughter seized with a fever and delirium, raving about her brother...let your feeling, Sir, suggest and plead for my inexpressible misery—a word from you like a voice from Heaven will save us from distraction and wretchedness. I am well informed General Washington reveres you character; say but to him that you wish my Son to be released and he will restore him to his distracted family, and render him to happiness.*

Vergennes brought the letter to Benjamin Franklin. The two diplomats had admired each other from the earliest days of Franklin's arrival in France. During their first meeting in December 1776, Franklin asked for French military aid and for France to actively join the war on America's side. Franklin held the admiration and respect of the diplomatic community and French citizenry alike.

Franklin was already aware of the Huddy/Asgill controversy from diplomatic reports and personal correspondences. The situation had blown up to engulf two continents: "The public prints all over Europe resounded with the unhappy catastrophe." People on both sides of the Atlantic anxiously awaited updates carried on arriving ships. Because reports lagged months behind actual events, frustration grew while everyone hoped for a fair solution.

Vergennes understood the personalities and tendencies of his royal patrons. He had worked closely with them for years, observing their proclivities and soft spots. He was the trusted confidant who had convinced Louis XVI to support the American Revolution. Vergennes saw the king as typically indecisive, but the foreign

Top: Charles Gravier, comte de Vergennes. *Library of Congress.*

Middle: King Louis XVI of France. *Public domain.*

Bottom: Marie Antoinette. *Public domain.*

From left to right: Peace commissioners John Jay, John Adams, Benjamin Franklin and Henry Laurens. William Temple Franklin is on the far right. *U.S. State Department.*

minister had lately taken note that Louis was more enamored than ever of Marie Antoinette. She had recently given birth to his long-awaited male heir, the Dauphin.

Unlike the French public, Vergennes had often witnessed the compassion of his queen, the doting mother, more empathetic than people thought (the insouciant statement famously associated with her was actually uttered by a princess a century earlier). Vergennes intuited that the queen could not help but relate to Lady Asgill.

It's easy to imagine Vergennes approaching Marie Antoinette at an opportune moment when she was alone. During a casual conversation, he'd mention something along the lines of, "I was speaking with Monsieur Franklin about a delicate letter I received from our countrywoman Sarah Theresa Pratviel, now the wife of a Baronet. She is very distressed to learn our friends the Americans are seeking to use her nineteen-year-old son as a kind of bargaining chip. The poor woman is worried her boy Charles might suffer a horrible fate. I have her tear-stained letter right here." Intrigued, the queen would want more details before bringing the foreign minister to her husband.

Louis XVI did not want to interfere in this contretemps until the queen—the infant Dauphin on her lap?—persuaded him otherwise. With Vergennes nodding agreement, Marie Antoinette suggested that the execution of Asgill by their American allies would reflect poorly on France. His Majesty would not want to jeopardize the peace talks underway in Paris, would he? *Bien sûr que non* (of course not). Vergennes was instructed to write immediately to George Washington.

Benjamin Franklin sent an urgent letter to Washington as well. It was vital for the American commander-in-chief to understand the French royals' concerns. The good Doctor Franklin was worried that the negotiations to end the war would fall apart should Asgill be sacrificed on the altar of vengeance.

Peace Talks in Peril

Benjamin Franklin, John Adams, John Jay and Henry Laurens had been meeting with their British counterparts at Versailles for months. The American peace commissioners (and their non-official advisor, Franklin's grandson, William Temple Franklin) were keen to find a resolution to the war in America. In the delicate dance between friends and adversaries, any misstep could jeopardize the peace talks. Best not to step on anyone's toes with the revenge killing of an innocent British officer.

Another serious practicality was that in gratitude for French aid during the war, the United States promised to sign a peace agreement with Britain only after France signed its own. The American Congress also mandated the commissioners to keep the French fully informed and "to undertake nothing in the negotiations for peace or truce without their knowledge or consent."

Vergennes wrote to Washington in August. Attaching Lady Asgill's poignant plea, the French minister appealed to Washington's decency as well as his vanity:

> *Madame Asgill has just wrote me* [that] *her son was the unhappy Victim destined by lot to expiate the odious Crime that a formal denial of Justice obliges you to revenge. Your Excellency will not read this Letter without being extremely affected. It had that effect upon the King and upon the Queen to whom I communicated it….I sincerely wish, Sir, that my intercession may meet success—the sentiment which dictates it & which you have not ceased to manifest on every occasion assures me that you will not be indifferent to the prayers & to the tears of a family who has recourse to your Clemency through me.*

Washington, increasingly uncomfortable, was open to any reasonable plan to delay Asgill's execution. He had communicated his private misgivings to the secretary of war: "Were I to give my private opinion respecting Asgill, I would pronounce in favor of his being released from his duress, and that he should be permitted to go to his friends in Europe."

During the five long months he waited on his destiny, Captain Asgill knew nothing of these intrigues and maneuverings. In his uninformed desperation, he wrote to Washington twice during the fall of 1782, urging him "to reflect on my unhappy Case, & to relieve me" and asking the general "to form an idea of my sufferings."

Washington hoped that Congress would solve his self-imposed predicament and relieve his burden of conscience. The members who favored retaliation for Huddy's death were content to let tensions simmer while they were busy creating governing documents for the new United States. Everyone was on tenterhooks.

Vergennes's letter didn't get to George Washington until the end of October. It reached the chambers of Congress the very day of a scheduled vote on Asgill. Members, caught completely off guard, questioned the authenticity of the letters and even Washington's signature on his cover letter. Satisfied that the documents were legitimate and astonished by the obvious unfairness to the young captain, Congress voted unanimously that sparing Asgill "should be given as a compliment to the King of France."

On November 13, Washington wrote to Captain Asgill, "It affords me singular pleasure to have it in my power to transmit you the inclosed [*sic*] Copy of an Act of Congress of the 7th instant, by which you are released from the disagreeable circumstances in which you have so long been—supposing you would wish to go into New York as soon as possible, I also inclose a passport for that purpose."

Freed

Liberated at last, Charles Asgill went to New York to meet briefly with Guy Carleton before sailing to England. In 1783, accompanied by his mother and two of his sisters, he traveled to Paris to offer personal thanks to the king and queen. Louis XVI and Marie Antoinette received them at the Palace of Fontainebleau. Charles was particularly happy to meet his savior, the comte de Vergennes. The young captain took the opportunity to visit with several of his former opponents in the American war, notably the Marquis de Lafayette, who'd commanded Continental troops for Washington at Yorktown.

George Washington (*left*) and Lafayette at Yorktown, October 1781. *Public domain.*

Nonetheless, Asgill held Washington responsible for the entire affair, not bothering to send any thanks to the American commander. Washington was miffed: "The treatment he met with, in my conception, merited an acknowledgment. None, however, was ever offered, and I never sought the cause." He recalled how he'd been filled "with the keenest anguish, I felt for him on many accounts."

Washington sent the welcomed news to Vergennes: "I think I may venture to assure your Excellency that your generous interposition had no small degree of Weight in procuring that decision....Capt. Asgill has been released and is at perfect liberty to return to the Arms of an affectionate parent whose pathetic address to your Excellency could not fail of interesting every feeling heart in her behalf."

Several international events (including a proposed mediation in Vienna, Austria, favored by Catherine the Great of Russia) might have derailed the negotiations in Paris, but the timely resolve of the Asgill controversy allowed the negotiators to overcome the last obstacle in their way. They agreed to a preliminary agreement ending the war on November 30, 1782. The official Treaty of Paris was signed ten months later.

American and British Perspectives

Any lingering resentments over the arduous affair should have faded with its satisfactory conclusion, but memories of the ordeal reverberated for years. Few of the principals or observers let go of the enormity of Joshua Huddy's execution in Highlands or Lippincott's acquittal.

The poet Philip Freneau from Middletown Point (Matawan) imagined a Loyalist who felt free to print whatever he chose, truth or libel:

I'll petition the rebels (if York is forsaken)
For a place in their Zion which ne'er shall be shaken;
I am sure they'll be clever: it seems their whole study:
They hung not young Asgill for old captain Huddy,
And it must be a truth that admits no denying,
If they spare us for murder they'll spare us for lying.

Home in England, Asgill was unable and unwilling to forget the mistreatment he suffered in confinement, speaking about it often and publicly.

Charles Asgill in England after his release. *Public domain.*

George Washington considered this a serious breach of etiquette. He had an aide-de-camp write a defense of his conduct to a Connecticut newspaper in 1786. The self-righteous letter conveniently left out Washington's egregious violation of the Articles of Capitulation.

Asgill, dismayed at another Washington insult, felt obliged to set the record straight in his reply to the *New-Haven Gazette and the Connecticut Magazine*:

> *Sir: In your Paper…the publication of some letters to & from* [General] *Washington together with parts of the Correspondence which passed during my Confinement in the Jerseys renders it necessary that I should make a few remarks on the insinuations in Washington's Letter, & give a fair account of the Treatment I received while I* [remained] *under the Singular circumstances in which Mr. Washington's judgment & feelings thought it justifiable & necessary to place.…I leave for the public to decide how far the treatment I have related deserved acknowledgements.…I could not with sincerity return thanks* [to Washington]*…my feelings would not allow me to give vent to reproaches.*

Image of a glorified George Washington. *New York Public Library.*

The postwar adoration of Washington had already gathered such fervor that the newspaper chose not to publish Asgill's rebuttal; 227 years would pass before the impassioned letter was discovered by an Asgill descendant. Anne Ammundsen, a Women's Royal Naval Service veteran, reprinted it in a 2023 book about the affair.

In 1788, Charles Asgill, 2nd Baronet, was appointed personal attendant to Frederick, Duke of York. His marriage to Jemima Ogle two years later produced no children. During his subsequent British military career, Asgill proved to be an effective career officer, eventually promoted to general. When he died without heirs in 1823, the Asgill baronetcy became extinct.

Thomas Paine brought the unsavory business back to life in 1788 when he republished *The American Crisis*. Paine's harsh criticism of Washington's "intended retaliation on Captain Asgill" reminded the soon-to-be first president, and his fellow citizens, of the last untoward aspect of the war.

Richard Lippincott After the War

After his acquittal in June 1782, Richard Lippincott went to England. Four years later, he petitioned the British Parliament for reimbursement, claiming that he "suffered losses worth £393...by reason of joining the Army of the King of Great Britain." His petition conveniently left out his 1782 court-martial defense that "the Associators should not be Viewed in the light of enlisted Soldiers."

Lippincott's claim was for horses, bed and bedding and some treasury notes, as well as debts he said he lost when he was renting a home in Shrewsbury. Parliament granted Lippincott three hundred acres in Toronto, Canada. He and his wife, Esther, lived there until her 1819 death. Lippincott survived for another seven years, applauded by his Toronto neighbors for his Loyalist activities. He is buried at Saint John's Cemetery on the Humber River. A street in nearby Harbord Village was named for him.

His grandson George T. Dennison tried his hand at revisionist history with the preposterous contention that "Captain Lippincott was naturally a person of the most harmless and quiet disposition....[Philip] White was half-brother to his wife...he was exasperated by the butchery of an innocent relative who was treated by Huddy as a spy."

Despite all the attention paid to the fascinating Huddy/Asgill episode during and immediately after the war, the world eventually forgot about Joshua Huddy. As for Colonel Tye, the man was barely noticed at all.

CHAPTER 17

BEATIFICATION, NEGLIGENCE AND REDEMPTION

He's a walkin' contradiction, partly truth and partly fiction.
—Kris Kristofferson

In December 1836, an old woman in Kentucky petitioned the U.S. Congress. A recent law had provided pensions for the widows of Revolutionary War soldiers, with the caveat that they married during the man's term of service. The provision made her ineligible, but she believed that she had a strong claim the august body could not ignore.

Martha Huddy Piatt's melancholic missive hit all the right notes:

> *Your petitioner appeals to the Justice of Congress. She is now seventy years of age…she alone survives to feel anew the horrors of that dreadful moment, when she was told she was fatherless, and that her gallant sire met the death of a malefactor; while his only crime was his ardent attachment to the cause of American liberty. The gratitude of the country has long been deferred, and though late, your petitioner asks…she may be allowed such sum in money, and such quantities of land as her father would have been entitled to, had he served until the conclusion of the revolutionary war.*

In February, a Congressional Committee agreed that there should be a "high estimate and grateful remembrance the service of Captain Joshua Huddy." A bill was proposed to grant his heirs three hundred acres and $1,200. Martha, his only living daughter, was hopeful, but nothing came of it. The House of Representatives introduced another bill in 1839, but it languished too. Martha Huddy Piatt died in 1842 without ever receiving compensation.

Nonetheless, the focus she had brought to her father ("who was not permitted to die a soldier's death") began the reappreciation of his heroic contributions sixty years prior.

The Hagiography of Joshua Huddy

Before Huddy's decrepit old home was torn down around 1856, the bullet holes on the walls and the burn marks on the door had been visible for three quarters of a century. However, the destruction of the house was not the end of the Joshua Huddy story.

Joel Parker, a Freehold politician and future governor of New Jersey, picked up the cause in 1858. *The Monmouth Democrat* reported his June 10 speech at a meeting of the New Jersey legislature at Thompson's Atlantic Pavilion in Highlands. With a pronounced florish, Parker pointed dramatically, intoning, "[Huddy] was taken to yonder point, and there suffered the ignominious death of the scaffold. He died as he lived, brave and unflinching." Huddy's hagiography had begun.

As the new country wove its mythology, authors found the Huddy/Tye story too emblematic to ignore. In 1861, John Barber and Henry Howe helped enshrine it. They introduced their two-volume history of the United States with this: "A trifling incident…which might be considered beneath the dignity of the historian to notice, is often of more value than whole pages of learned inferences or glowing descriptions."

Barber and Howe's portrayal of the war in Monmouth County was anything but trivial. They devoted the better part of three pages just to our protagonists, including the first known illustration of Huddy's Colts Neck house. The two historians began the treatment with the siege ("One evening, in the summer of 1780, a party of about 60 refugees, commanded by Tye, a mulatto, attacked [Huddy's] dwelling.") and concluded with the resolution of the Asgill affair ("The lovers of humanity rejoiced that the necessity of retaliation was superseded."). Fact and fiction were melding.

A flurry of articles appeared in 1873. Colonel Tye was featured in the September 11 edition of *The Monmouth Democrat*:

> *Titus or Col. Tye as he was commonly called, usually commanded a mongrel crew of negroes and tories. He died of lockjaw, occasioned by the wound in his wrist. He was a slave of John Corlies, and was born and bred in the south part of this township. He was an honorable, brave, but headstrong man. Several acts of generosity are remembered of him, and he was justly more respected as an enemy than many of his brethren of a fairer complexion.*

His rough-edged militiaman foe was elevated to sainthood by this headline in the *Monmouth Inquirer* of November 6: "CAPTAIN JOSHUA HUDDY, THE HERO MARTYR OF OLD MONMOUTH."

The *Army and Navy Journal* printed a July 1876 article replete with inaccuracies about the events of 1782:

> *Another incident which preceded and hastened the fate of Capt. Tigh* [sic] *was an act that, at the time, excited the sympathy and sorrow of every patriot throughout the land....Over his* [Huddy's] *grave many an oath was taken to follow his murderers, and it became well understood in time that the notorious Tigh was among those connected with the base deed.*

Tye, of course, was dead for two years when Huddy was hanged.

Before widespread news syndication, Huddy stories showed up in newspapers far from Monmouth County, places such as Charleston, South Carolina, and Waterstown, Wisconsin. They were usually published during community celebrations of Revolutionary anniversaries, the Fourth of July or the British surrender at Yorktown.

Military historian William S. Stryker wrote about Huddy after he attended a Toms River Blockhouse centennial service in 1883. Two years after that, Huddy and Tye gained widespread recognition resulting from the Franklin Ellis publication *History of Monmouth County, New Jersey*. Edwin Salter and George Beekman accelerated the trend with their popular *Old Times in Old Monmouth* (1887). Contradictory or imaginary details of the Huddy/Tye rivalry became accepted truth.

As stories proliferated, each new wave of interest enhanced the legends. The merged *Freehold Transcript and the Monmouth Inquirer* ran dozens of Huddy articles well into the early twentieth century. When the *Evening Post* of New York printed, "Huddy, The Patriot Martyr. The True Story" in 1898, our militia captain was firmly fixed in the American Pantheon as beau idéal.

Where Was the Blockhouse?

The Toms River Chapter of the Daughters of the American Revolution began an effort to erect a Huddy monument at the blockhouse site in 1893. Remnants of the fort had long since been covered over, but an elderly resident claimed that he'd seen its deteriorated stumps when he was a boy. The old fort was up a slight rise from the river, near Washington Street. The DAR plaque marked the site before the original location was obliterated by the construction of the Toms River Town Hall in 1902 and the Ocean County Library in 1925.

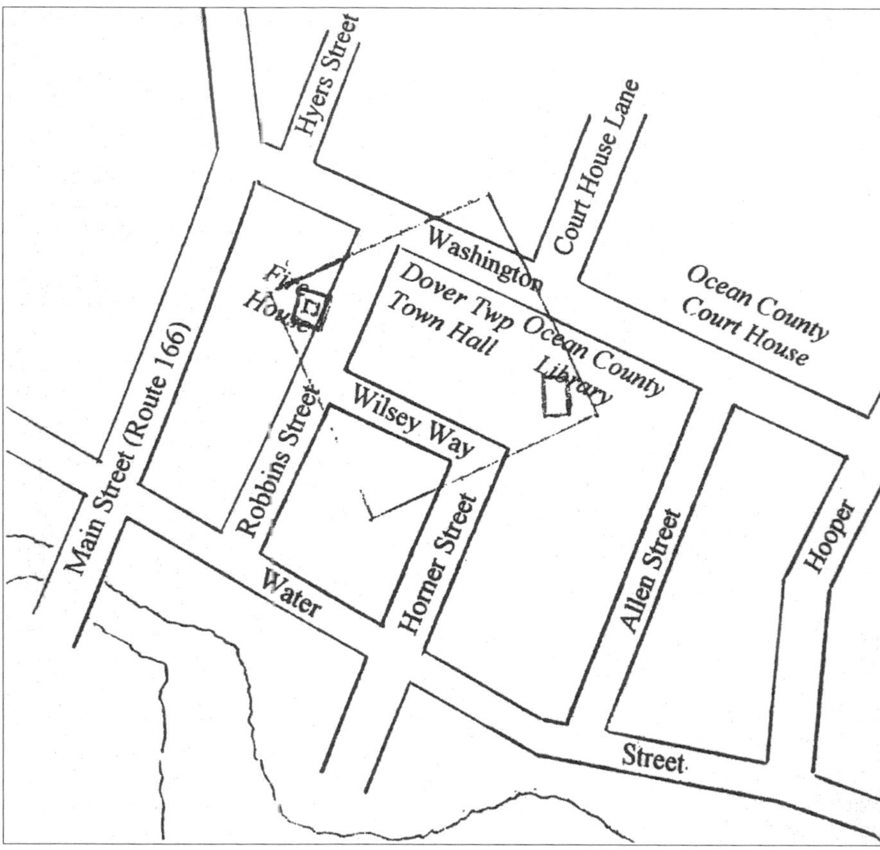

The blockhouse (outline) was on the site of today's town hall and Ocean County Library. *Collection of the Ocean County Historical Society.*

CAPTAIN JOSH HUDDY
APRIL 12, 1782

The Britishers at Sandy Hook, they think they're mighty big,
(Each soger with his bright red coat, gloves, stock an' powdered wig);
They've lots of ships, an' lots of guns, an' men a-plenty, too–
They never scairt Josh Huddy, with all their hullaballoo;
An' ef they left their ships-o'-war to foray on the land,
They al'ays had to reckon with his Monmouth County band.

It won't be long 'fore we ketch'em,
'Fore we ketch that Tory gang–
A Refugee's good as a Pine Robber,
And a Pine Robber's good for to hang!

Dick Lippincott an' Cap'n Tie, the Whites an' that hull gang,
More'n oncet they swore that 'fore the dawn they'd see Josh Huddy hang;
But when the Refugees an' Reg'lars scoured the country round
They's apt to find the sly ol'fox had turned into a hound–
Afore they'd git back to their boats Josh Huddy's turn come then,
An' he would hunt the hunters with his Monmouth County men.

They ketch'd him at Toms River Bridge, when they was five to one–
But all them odds agin him didn't make Josh Huddy run.
Each Tory had a musket, an' each Jarsey lad a pike–
We laid 'em out a man for man afore we ceas'd to strike–
With numbers they outfou't us, we could stand no longer, then
They captur'd Cap'n Huddy of the Monmouth County men.

They took him from his prison ship out to his native shore–
(They knew it was plain murder; they call'd it an act of war)
His gallus was three fence rails, pointin' up'ards to the sky;
But Cap'n Huddy show'd 'em how a Jarsey boy could die.
They left his corpse a-hangin' as they hurried from the strand,
His corpse, to call for vengeance, to his Monmouth County band.

Now Bastard Billy Franklin, an' Dick Lippincott, an' crew,
We've smoked you out of Jarsey to your Tory rendezvous;

An'-lest ye think that we've forgot you an' Your hellish work,

Above: William H. Fischer published this poem about Huddy in 1906. *Public domain.*

Opposite: The commemorative blockhouse plaque on Robbins Street next to Toms River Town Hall. *Rick Geffken.*

Written in Verse and Stone

The Town of Toms River purchased some reclaimed land on marshy Gowdy Island in 1905. While delays and deliberations stalled plans for a public space, William H. Fisher published "Captain Josh Huddy" in 1906 to boost the effort. Written in an imagined eighteenth-century Jersey patois, the poem added to the already broad acceptance of many legends about the man.

The park's memorial to Captain Huddy and his militiamen was dedicated in 1931. Today, Huddy Park and its replica blockhouse hug the riverfront, downhill from the original location.

The Huddy memorial and replica blockhouse in Toms River. *Rick Geffken.*

WHERE WAS JOSHUA HUDDY ACTUALLY HANGED?

The location of Huddy's demise was almost lost forever. Two months after he died, the *Freeman's Journal or the North-American Intelligencer* reported:

> *On the ridge of the mountains commonly called Neversink hills in Monmouth County, East Jersey, a considerable quantity of land, some say forty acres, gave way in April last, and sunk down a considerable depth. It is supposed by the country people thereabouts, to have been occasioned by the washing and undermining of the sea, to which it is contiguous. It is somewhat remarkable, that the sunken land was only at a small distance from the spot where the unfortunate Capt. Huddy suffered death; and took its present situation but a very short time thereafter.*

For more than one hundred years after Huddy's death, the residents of Highlands held a certain tree in high regard. Used for his execution, the "Joshua Huddy Tree" grew tall above the south side of Water Witch Avenue until it eventually toppled over. When the railroad went through, its tracks

Top: The two men on the left are standing where Joshua Huddy was hanged. *Walter Guenther*.

Bottom: The first location of the Highlands Huddy Memorial. *From the* Asbury Park Press.

skirted the site. (Barber and Howe were the first to suggest that Huddy died beneath a gallows of three upright fence rails. This version of his death seems far-fetched—those rails would have been extremely long.)

By the early twentieth century, tons of dredge spoil from the Shrewsbury River channel had covered the marshy tidal areas in the northern section of Highlands. The sand created new building lots, which encouraged more permanent residents and attracted more summertime visitors. The Huddy hanging site was then five hundred yards from the river and also more accessible to everyone.

Borough of Highlands officials were eager for the town's growth in the early twentieth century. Staking a claim to Huddy glory could only help. The *Red Bank Register* and the *Asbury Park Press* applauded the idea of a memorial, but years passed as plans were formulated and changed.

In 1910, the Central Railroad Company donated a right of way and a granite stone to the Sons of the American Revolution. Edward S. Atwood of the Monmouth County Historical Association superintended the memorial project from his home in the exclusive Water Witch Club (Monmouth Hills) community overlooking the site.

Dana Howell and Joe Zemla of the Monmouth County Historical Association at the Huddy monument in 2025. *Rick Geffken.*

At completion, the stone and pedestal were enclosed by a metal pipe fence where the tree had stood. The two-foot-square inscribed bronze tablet read:

> *Here Captain Joshua Huddy of the Monmouth County Artillery, a Prisoner of War captured March 24, 1782 while defending the Block House at Toms River was hung by Tories without warrant April 12, 1782. The British authorities repudiated but did not atone for that crime. The Sons of the Revolution in New Jersey have set up this stone to the memory of the patriotic victim.*

Two years after World War II, the American Legion petitioned the borough to move the neglected monument down Water Witch Avenue to a more accessible greenspace. In 1948, Highlands dedicated Huddy Park, where the monument remains today.

The Water Witch Development Company named a nearby street Huddy Avenue in 1950.

Bicentennial

As his military exploits and martyrdom became more widely known, so too did veneration of Joshua Huddy, peaking during the 200th anniversary of the founding of the United States. When the Tall Ships fleet anchored inside Sandy Hook during the bicentennial celebrations in 1976, the grand pageantry of flags and pennants flying high above the waters of the Shrewsbury rekindled Revolutionary fervor among Americans everywhere.

The Tall Ships were a resolute reminder of all the eighteenth-century vessels loaded with thousands of British sailors and soldiers whose first view of the American colonies was the Sandy Hook Lighthouse. The same view was familiar and ultimately deadly for Joshua Huddy.

Bicentennial symposia, dinners, balls and re-creations of battles celebrated the nation's founding throughout Monmouth County. Bob Schoeffling, president of the Atlantic Highlands Historical Society, spoke to audiences about the rivalry between the Huddy and Tye. Markers were installed at Hart's Tavern, the Hart/Huddy Colts Neck home and the scene of his tangle with the British as they retreated from Monmouth Court House.

Huddy marker at Colts Neck Memorial Park. *Rick Geffken.*

More Recognition

In 2004, the Monmouth County Archives, a division of the Monmouth County Clerk's Office, hosted its annual Archives & History Day. Archivist Gary Saretzky curated "The Joshua Huddy Era: Documents of the American Revolution," which publicized a plethora of primary source documents.

Tye Belatedly Acknowledged

For two centuries, Tye was portrayed as a bit player on the fringes of Monmouth County history, a foil for the glorified Huddy. Understandably. Why celebrate a man who fought against our revered Patriots as they struggled to establish a new nation? Few people knew about, and fewer wanted to believe in, Black Revolutionary heroes. Besides, enslavement was the shameful legacy of the southern states. Let's not bring up a runaway from New Jersey.

Depending on the author and when the stories were written, Tye was variously described as a scout, a guide, the leader or the commander of the Black Brigade and mixed bands of Refugees. Some said that Tye's was merely a supporting role in military operations led by white officers. The discrepancies can be reconciled by considering who wrote the contrary narratives.

The rebels probably exaggerated the military acumen of runaways. Many enslavers depicted their former chattel as particularly primitive opponents, "insurgent extensions of British power." Not for nothing do we read about mongrel crews and wild men rampaging and terrorizing white citizens.

The British had their reasons to minimize the contributions of the very same runaways fighting for them. His Majesty's professional army was proud to portray white officers as superior leaders, at the same time begrudgingly and infrequently mentioning Black troops performing their grunt work. The eyes of the beholders only saw so far.

Edwin Salter's 1890 comment was the singular recognition of Tye's dedication to his cause: "Like our forefathers, he fought for his liberty, which our ancestors unfortunately refused to give him."

In 1896, a retired military officer and lawyer born in Manasquan wrote about the war in which his same-named ancestor became famous. Colonel Ethan Allen had this to say about a Black fighter for the British:

> *Wherever Tigh went, the torch and knife did their work upon the defenceless families, whose guardians were in the camp with Washington. It was difficult to overtake the robber, for his work was done in a twinkle, and he and his band being intimately acquainted with the country, easily placed themselves beyond pursuit.*

More years would pass before more nuanced studies of Tye appeared. The history of the United States is not, as our monuments and some politicians suggest, written in stone, but refined as scholars reexamine and reinterpret primary documents.

Books about slavery in the United States appeared before the Civil War, notably the 1845 autobiography *Narrative of the Life of Frederick Douglass*. Most published works were about slavery in the South, not in New Jersey, where enslavement had been literally whitewashed from our history.

Alex Haley's 1976 book *Roots*, and the television miniseries one year later, exposed enslavement to the American public with personal stories few could ignore. *Roots*, despite criticism of Haley's inaccuracies, opened the door to deeper studies of Black history. (Forty-three years later, The

1619 Project in the *New York Times Magazine* was similarly assailed by revanchist traditionalists.)

Graham Russell Hodges's writings did much to raise awareness about the extent of slavery in New Jersey. Michael Adelberg's archival investigations provided insights into people neglected in traditional histories. Their books and articles about eighteenth-century Monmouth County showed how and why the runaway Titus became the Refugee Colonel Tye.

The Public Broadcasting System aired a Colonel Tye segment in the four-part series *Africans in America* in October 1998. The story of the runaway who rose to prominence reached a national audience.

The Sandy Hook Foundation, in cooperation with the New Jersey Historical Commission, the National Park Service and the National Park Foundation, is in the process of creating an innovative project telling the story of Colonel Tye to be featured at Sandy Hook. As of this writing, the on-site immersive experience, which may feature augmented reality–based walking tours and interactive exhibits, is expected to open at the Gateway National Recreational Area, Sandy Hook, New Jersey, in the coming years. (The Sandy Hook Visitor Center at 732-872-5970 can provide information about admission fees and visiting schedules at the park. More is available at Gateway's website, https://www.nps.gov/gate.)

America's 250th birthday on July 4, 2026, will be observed throughout the United States, New Jersey, Monmouth County and its many communities. The MonmouthNJ 250 Committee was formed by the Monmouth County Board of County Commissioners in 2023 to coordinate the county's commemoration of America's birthday and its significant role in the fight for independence. The committee has worked to highlight and honor the people, places and events that have made Monmouth County a special place to live, work, play in and visit for more than two and a half centuries. Connect via Monmouth County 250 (https://monmouthnj250.org) to learn more about the many anniversary celebrations of this momentous occasion, sign up for an e-mail newsletter and follow on social media (@Monmouthnj250).

Why Do They Matter?

Colonel Tye and the Captain Joshua Huddy probed ideas of freedom and independence dissimilarly, yet their discrete aspirations were more aligned the closer we look. The former refused to be owned and controlled; the latter rejected conformity and rule by others. They were committed Revolutionaries, uniquely American.

Thomas Jefferson's "All men are created equal" was the audacious hypothesis for the American Experiment. Several monumental battles and hundreds of scrums field-tested it. The country that arose 250 years ago is still evaluating the results.

As the grateful heirs to the people whose sacrifices bestowed so much, we manifestly espouse their ideals. In this light, because Tye chose the losing side, he can seem less worthy of attention than Huddy, whose compatriots triumphed. None can doubt that the militiaman was valorous, but the runaway slave was gallant, too, because he represents precisely what Jefferson's pronouncement declares.

Reinterpretations of long-held historical beliefs are fraught but freeing in the fullness of time. We're reminded that Jefferson also affirmed:

> *The flames kindled on the 4th of July, 1776, have spread across too much of the globe to be extinguished by the feeble engines of despotism; on the contrary, they will consume the engines and all who work them.*

BIBLIOGRAPHY

Adelberg, Michael. *The American Revolution in Monmouth County: The Theatre of Spoil and Destruction*. The History Press, 2010.

———. Database of the American Revolution in Monmouth County, New Jersey. Monmouth County Historical Association Archives, 1996.

———. "The Forgotten First Battle of Monmouth." *Journal of the American Revolution* (2013).

———. "'Long in Hand and Altogether Fruitless': The Pennsylvania Salt Works and Salt-Making on the New Jersey Shore during the American Revolution in Pennsylvania History." *Pennsylvania History: A Journal of Mid-Atlantic Studies* 80, no. 2 (2013).

———. *Roster of the People of Revolutionary Monmouth County (New Jersey)*. Clearfield, 1997.

———. *Salt Making*. Rutgers University, 2015.

———. "The Transformation of Local Governance in Monmouth County, New Jersey, during the War of the American Revolution." *Journal of the Early Republic* 31, no. 3 (2011).

Aders, Magdalena. *Your Majesty, Your Crown*. Christ Church, 1988.

Allen, Ethan. *United States Army and Navy Journal, and Gazette of the Regular and Volunteer Forces*. Vol. 13, *1875–76*. Unknown publisher, 1876.

Almon, J.A. *Candid and Impartial Narrative of the Fleet under the Command of Lord Howe*. Privately printed, 1779.

Alt, William E., and Betty Sowers Alt. *Black Soldiers, White Wars: Black Warriors from Antiquity to the Present*. Praeger, 2002.

American Battlefield Trust. "William Franklin." https://www.battlefields.org/learn/biographies/william-franklin.

American Philosophical Society and Yale University. The Papers of Benjamin Franklin. Yale University Press, 2011.

American Revolution. Podcast. https://blog.amrevpodcast.com.

Ammundsen, Anne. *The Charles Asgill Affair: Setting the Record Straight*. Heritage Books, 2023.

Ancestry.com. American Loyalist Claims, 1776–1835.

———. Corlies Family genealogy.

———. Fold3 military records.

Anderson, Robert C., George F. Sanborn Jr. and Melinde Lutz Sanborn. *The Great Migration: Immigrants to New England, 1634–1635*. New England Historic Genealogical Society, 1999.

Applegate, James Bennett. *An Applegate Saga: A Line of Descent from Thomas the Immigrant*. Privately printed, 2015.

Armstrong, William Clinton, ed. *Patriotic Poems of New Jersey*. New Jersey Society Sons of the American Revolution, 1906.

Bancroft, George. *History of the United States from the Discovery of the American Continent*. Vol. 2. Chas. Little and James Brown, 1841.

Barber, John Warner, and Henry Howe. *Historical Collections of New Jersey: Past and Present*. Privately printed, 1868.

———. *Our Whole Country: Or the Past and Present of the United States*. Vol. 1. George F. Tuttle and Henry M'Cauley, 1861.

Barsa, Diane. *The Asgill Affair*. Ocean County Historical Society. Privately printed, 2021.

Beagrie, Neil. "Early Huddys in Cornwall, Ireland, and North America." Genealogy, 2004. genealogy.com.

Becker, Carl L. *The Eve of the Revolution: A Chronicle of the Breach with England*. Yale University Press, 1918.

Beekman, George Crawford. *Early Dutch Settlers of Monmouth County, New Jersey*. Moreau Bros., 1901.

Berlet, Diane, and Graem Coles. *The Loyalist Tiles of St. Alban's: Encaustic Memorial Tiles of the 19th Century*. St. Alban's Church, 2011.

Bilby, Joseph G. *New Jersey: A Military History*. Westholme Publishing, 2017.

Bilby, Joseph G., James M. Madden and Harry Ziegler. *350 Years of New Jersey History*. The History Press, 2014.

Bill, Alfred Hoyt. *New Jersey and the Revolutionary War*. D. Van Nostrand Company, 1964.

Black Loyalists: Our History, Our People. Canada's Digital Collections. https://blackloyalist.com/cdc.

Booraem, Hendrik. "Abraham Carlisle and John Roberts Trials, 1778." Encyclopedia. https://www.encyclopedia.com/law/law-magazines/abraham-carlisle-and-john-roberts-trials-1778.

Boyd, Paul D. "Settlers Along the Shores: Lenape Spatial Patterns in Coastal Monmouth County, 1670–1750." Vols. 1 and 2. Dissertation, Rutgers University, 2005.

Boyer, Charles S. "Old Ferries, Camden, New Jersey: An Address Delivered Before the Camden County Historical Society." Privately printed, 1921.

Braddock-Rogers, Kennet. *Saltworks of New Jersey during the American Revolution*. American Chemical Society, 1938.

Braisted, Todd. "The Black Pioneers and Others: The Military Role of Black Loyalists in the American War for Independence." Academia. https://www.academia.edu/42861545/Todd_W_Braisted_The_Black_Pioneers_and_Others_The_Military_Role_of_Black_Loyalists_in_the_American_War_for_Independence.

———. On-Line Institute for Advanced Loyalist Studies. https://www.royalprovincial.com/index.htm.

———. "Such as Are Absolutely Free: Benjamin Thompson's Black Dragoons." *Journal of the American Revolution* (February 2021).

Brannon, Rebecca. *Loyalists and the American Revolution*. Oxford University Press, 2021.

Breen, T.H., and Stephen Foster. "Moving to the New World: The Character of Early Massachusetts Immigration." *William and Mary Quarterly* 30, no. 2 (1973).

Bunce, Oliver Bell. *The Romance of the Revolution: Being a History of the Personal Adventures, Heroic Exploits, and Romantic Incidents, as Enacted in the War of Independence*. Bunce & Brother, 1853.

Bunnell, Fred G. *Captain Joshua Huddy: The Hero of Toms River*. Ocean County Bureau of Publicity, 1941.

Bushnell, I. Charles. *Narrative of the Exertions and Sufferings of Lieut. James Moody, in Cause of Government Since the Year 1776*. Privately printed, 1865.

Butler, John P. *Index, The Papers of the Continental Congress, 1774–1789*. Vol. 4. National Archives and Records Service, 1978.

Carey, Charles W., Jr. "Lord Dunmore's Ethiopian Regiment." Thesis, Virginia Polytechnic Institute, 1995.

Child, Theodore. "Washington on the French Stage." *Lippincott's Magazine of Popular Literature and Science* (1882).

Chopra, Ruma. *Choosing Sides: Loyalists in Revolutionary America*. Rowman & Littlefield Publishers, 2013.

Clark, Mary Sherrerd. *In the Olden Days: Papers Colonial and Revolutionary*. Privately printed, 1905.

Clinton, Sir Henry. *The American Rebellion: Sir Henry Clinton's Narrative of His Campaigns, 1775–1782*. Yale University Press, 1954.

Coggins, Jack. *Ships and Seamen of the American Revolution*. Dover Publications, 1969.

Corliss, Augustus W. *A Genealogical Record of the Corliss Family of America*. Privately printed, 1875.

Corwin, Edward Tanjore. *A Manual of the Reformed Church in America, 1627–1902*. Board of Publication of the Reformed Church in America, 1902.

Coughlin, Bill. "The British Attack Toms River, Toms River Blockhouse." Historical Marker Database. https://www.hmdb.org/m.asp?m=139167.

Covington, Richard. "Marie Antoinette." *Smithsonian Magazine*. https://www.smithsonianmag.com/history/Marie-Antoinette -134629573.

Craig, H. Stanley. *Burlington County New Jersey Marriages*. Gloucester County Historical Society, 1977.

———. *Salem County New Jersey Genealogical Data*. Vol. 1. Gloucester County Historical Society, 1980.

Crawford, Michael J., ed. *Naval Documents of the American Revolution*. Vol. 12. Department of the Navy, 2013.

Cunningham, John T. *Chatham at the Crossing of the Fishawack*. Chatham Historical Society, 1967.

Damon, Allan J. "The Melancholy Case of Captain Asgill." *American Heritage* (February 1970).

Dandridge, Anne S. *The Forman Genealogy*. Forman-Bassett-Hatch Company, 1903.

Dandridge, Danske. *American Prisoners of the Revolution*. Michie Company Printers, 1911.

Davidson, Stephen. "Unpacking an Execution Notice." *Loyalist Trails* (2017). United Empire Loyalist Association of Canada.

De Monte, Anthony. *A Short History of the Life of Captain "Jack" Joshua Huddy*. Privately printed, n.d.

DeMoss-Caughron, Edith Susanna. *Maternal Ancestral Lines of Edith Susanna DeMoss-Caughron by Herself*. Privately printed, 1950.

Denwick, Sarah A. *Ancestry of John S. Gustin and His Wife Susan McComb*. David Clapp, 1900.

Dodyk, Delight W. "Troublesome Times A-Coming: The American Revolution and New Jersey Women." In Mitnick, *New Jersey in the American Revolution*. Rutgers University Press, 2005.

DuBois, William E., and Patterson DuBois. *Bi-Centenary Reunion of the Descendants of Louis and Jacques Du Bois (Emigrants to America, 1660 and 1675) at New Paltz, New York, 1875*. Rue & Jones, 1876.

Duess, Marie Murphy. *Colonial Inns and Taverns of Bucks County: How Pubs, Taprooms and Hostelries Made Revolutionary History*. The History Press, 2007.

Dustin, Logan. *Joshua Huddy: A Symbolic Figure for Monmouth County During the War for Independence*. Monmouth University, 2013.

Ecelbarger, Gary. *George Washington's Momentous Year: Twelve Months that Transformed the Revolution*. Vol. 1. *The Philadelphia Campaign*. Westholme Publishing, 2004.

Ehrensberger, Wayne C. "Cutlope Hancock's Military Service." Armstrong County Genealogy Club, 2017. https://acgclub.info/?page_id=379.

Ellis, Franklin. *History of Monmouth County, New Jersey*. R.T. Peck & Company, 1885.

Elwell, Bonny Beth. *Upper Pittsgrove, Elmer, and Pittsgrove*. Arcadia Publishing, 2013.

Farner, Thomas P. "Exchange." *The Sandpaper*, 1982.

———. "Huddy Hangs." *The Sandpaper*, 1982.

Federal Writers' Project. *New Jersey: A Guide to Its Present and Past*. Viking Press, 1939.

———. *The WPA Guide to Pennsylvania, The Keystone State*. University of Pennsylvania, 1940.

Finn, Donald F.X. *Bibliography of Materials Relating to Captain Joshua Huddy and the Huddy-Asgill Affair*. Twin Lights Press, 1978.

Fischer, William H. Biographical Cyclopedia of Ocean County, New Jersey. H.O. Smith, 1899.

———. *Toms River Block House Fight, March 24, 1782*. Ocean County Historical Society, 1973.

Fitzpatrick, John J. *The Writings of George Washington*. Vol. 23. U.S. Government Printing Office, 1939.

Fold3. United States Military Records, 2024. Via Ancestry.com.

Force, Peter. *American Archives: Consisting of a Collection of Authentick Records, State Papers, Debates, and Letters and Other Notices of Publick Affairs*. Washington, D.C., 1848.

Forman, Charles. *Three Revolutionary Soldiers: David Forman, Jonathan Forman, Thomas Marsh Forman*. Forman-Bassett-Hatch Company, 1902.

Forman, Samuel A. *Ill-Fated Frontier: Peril and Possibilities in the Early American West*. Littlefield, 2021.

Fowler, David J. *Egregious Villains, Wood Robbers, and London Traders: The Pine Robber Phenomenon in New Jersey During the Revolutionary War*. Rutgers University, 1987.

Franklin, John Hope, and Alfred A. Moss. *From Slavery to Freedom: A History of Negro Americans*. Knopf, 1947.

Fraser, Antonia. *Marie Antoinette: The Journey*. Anchor Books, 2001.

Freehold Township. https://www.twp.freehold.nj.us/436/History-of-the-Village-of-West-Freehold.

Freeman, Douglas Southall. *George Washington, a Biography: Victory with the Help of France*. University of Michigan, 1981.

Gabrielan, Randall. *Middletown Township*. Vol. 2. Arcadia Publishing, 1995.

Gabriele, Michael C. *Colonial Taverns of New Jersey*. The History Press, 2023.

Gagan, David. *The Denison Family of Toronto, 1792–1925*. University of Toronto Press, 1973.

Gall, Michael J. *A Hill on the Periphery: New Insights on the Battle of Monmouth, June 28, 1778*. Richard Grubb & Associates Inc., 2019.

Gall, Michael J., and Richard F. Veit. *Archaeologies of African American Life in the Upper Mid-Atlantic*. University of Alabama Press, 2017.

Garlick, Reverend Bernard McKean. *A History of St. Peter's Church, Freehold, New Jersey, 1702–1967*. Privately printed, 1967.

Geffken, Rick. *Stories of Slavery in New Jersey*. The History Press, 2021.

Geffken, Rick, and Muriel J. Smith. *Hidden History of Monmouth County*. The History Press, 2019.

George Washington Papers. Series 4, General Correspondence: Alexander Scammel, Report on Negroes in the Continental Army, 1778. Library of Congress.

Gerlach, Larry R. *New Jersey in the American Revolution, 1763–1783: A Documentary History*. New Jersey Historical Commission, 1975.

———. *Prologue to Independence: New Jersey in the Coming of the American Revolution*. Rutgers University Press, 1976.

Gigantino, James J., ed. *The American Revolution in New Jersey: Where the Battlefront Meets the Home Front*. Rutgers University Press, 2015.

Gigantino, James John. "Freedom and Unfreedom in the 'Garden of America': Slavery and Abolition in New Jersey, 1770–1857." Dissertation, University of Georgia, 2010.

———. *The Ragged Road to Abolition: Slavery and Freedom in New Jersey, 1775–1865*. University of Pennsylvania Press, 2014.

Gilbert, Alan. *Black Patriots and Loyalists: Fighting for Emancipation in the War for Independence*. University of Chicago Press, 2012.

Gilje, Paul A., and William Pencak, eds. *New York in the Age of the Constitution, 1775–1800*. New York Historical Society, 1992.

Glenn, Thomas Allen. *William Churchill Houston, 1746–1788*. Privately printed, 1903.

Gordon-Reed, Annette. *The Hemingses of Monticello: An American Family*. W.W. Norton & Company, 2008.

Gordon, Thomas F. *The History of New Jersey from Its Discovery by Europeans to the Adoption of the Federal Constitution*. Daniel Fenton, 1834.

Graham, James J. *The Life of General Daniel Morgan of the Virginia Line of the Army of the United States*. New York, 1856.

———. *Memoir of General Graham*. Privately printed, 1862.

Greene, Nathanael, Richard K. Showman and Dennis Michael Conrad. *The Papers of General Nathanael Greene, December 1766–December 1776*. University of Michigan, 1976.

Greene, Walter Anson, and Ella Louise Geib Greene. *Supplement to the Greene Family of St. Albans, Vermont: With Added Sections on Some Branches of the Rhode Island Greenes Who Settled in Michigan, New Jersey, Pennsylvania, Vermont, Wisconsin*. Privately printed, 1969.

Green, Howard L., ed. *Words that Make New Jersey History. New Jersey Historical Commission*. Rutgers University Press, 1994.

Griffith, Lee Ellen. *Freehold*. Arcadia Publishing, 1996.

Grumet, Robert S. *The Munsee Indians: A History*. University of Oklahoma, 2009.

Guthorn, Peter J. *British Maps of the American Revolution*. Philip Freneau Press, 1972.

Haines, George, and Richard Haines. *Ancestry of Haines and Allied Families*. S. Crew and Sons Company, 1902.

Hannings, Bud. *Chronology of the American Revolution, Military and Political Actions Day by Day*. McFarland & Company, 2008.

Hannum, Patrick H. "Book Review: A Perfect Frenzy: A Royal Governor, His Black Allies, and the Crisis that Spurred the American Revolution." All Things Liberty, February 2025. https://allthingsliberty.com/2025/02/a-perfect-frenzy-a-royal-governor-his-black-allies-and-the-crisis-that-spurred-the-american-revolution.

Hayden, Reverend Horace Edwin. *A Brief Sketch of Captain Joseph Davis and Lieutenant William Jones*. Wyoming Historical and Geological Society, 1897.

Henderson, Helen. *Matawan and Aberdeen of Town and Field*. Arcadia Publishing, 2003.

Henriques, Peter R. *First and Always: A New Portrait of George Washington*. University of Virginia, 2020.

Herpich, Robert F. *Gravelly Point Remembrances, Highlands, New Jersey, 1916–1935*. Privately printed, 1991.

Heston, Alfred Miller. *South Jersey: A History, 1664–1924*. Lewis Historical Publishing, 1924.

Heyl, Reverend Francis. *The Battle of Germantown*. City History Society of Philadelphia, 1908.

Hillpern, Edmund P. "The Minimum Quaker." *Friends Journal* (1967).

Hills, George M. *History of the Church in Burlington, New Jersey*. W.S. Sharp, 1876.

Hinshaw, William Wade. *American Quaker Genealogy*. Vol. 2. Genealogical Publishing Company, 1938.

Hirshfeld, Fritz. *George Washington and Slavery, a Documentary Portrayal*. University of Missouri Press, 1997.

Historical Manuscripts Commission of Great Britain. Report on American Manuscripts in the Royal Institution of Great Britain, 1972.

Historical Society of Pennsylvania. *Pennsylvania Magazine of History and Biography* 9 (1885).

History of Monmouth County, New Jersey, 1664–1920. Vol. 3. Lewis Publishing Company, 1922.

Hodges, Graham R. *African Americans in Monmouth County during the American Revolution*. Monmouth County Park System, 1990.

———. *Black New Jersey, 1664 to the Present Day*. Rutgers University Press, 2019.

———. *Root & Branch: African Americans in New York & East Jersey*. University of North Carolina Press, 1999.

———. *Slavery and Freedom in the Rural North: African Americans in Monmouth County, New Jersey, 1665–1865*. Rowman & Littlefield Publishing, 1997.

———. *Slavery, Freedom & Culture Among Early American Workers*. M.E. Sharpe, 1998.

Hodges, Graham, Russell Gao and Alan Edward Brown, eds. *"Pretends to Be Free": Runaway Slave Advertisements from Colonial and Revolutionary New York and New Jersey*. 25th Anniversary Edition. Fordham University Press, 2019.

Hollander, J.H. "The Naturalization of Jews in the American Colonies Under the Act of 1740." *American Jewish Historical Society Journal*, no. 5 (1897).

Honeyman, A. Van Doren, ed. *New Jersey Law Journal* 27 (1904). New Jersey Law Journal Publishing.

———. *Proceedings of the New Jersey Historical Society*. New Jersey Historical Society, 1926.

Horner, William S. *This Old Monmouth of Ours*. Moreau Brothers, 1932.

Hotten, John Camden. *The Original Lists of Persons of Quality…Who Went from Great Britain to the American Plantations, 1600–1700*. J.W. Bouton, 1874.

Hyde, Mary C. Murray. "Battle of Navesink." *New York Times*, 1896.

———. "Captain Huddy and the Fall of the North Ministry." *Spirit of '76* (November 1898).

———. Private correspondences, courtesy of the Beekman Family, 2024.

———. "Retreat After the Battle of Monmouth." *Spirit of '76* (August 1899).

Jaquett, Josephine, and Elmer VanNam. *Place Names of Salem County, N.J.* Salem County Historical Society, 1964.

Jefferson, Thomas. *The Papers of Thomas Jefferson*. Princeton University Press, 1974.

Jenkins, Alexander. *The History and Description of the City of Exeter: And Its Environs, Ancient and Modern, Civil and Ecclesiastical.* P. Hedgeland, 1806.

Jewish Heritage Museum of Monmouth County, Freehold, New Jersey.

Jewish Historical Society. *Publications of the American Jewish Historical Society*, no. 17 (1909).

Jews in Colonial America. AJHS Oppenheim Collection, 1650–1850, Folder (05), Gomperts, Gompert S.—Hart, Solomon.

Johnston, Henry Phelps. *The Campaign of 1776 Around New York and Brooklyn*. Long Island Historical Society, 1878.

Jones, Edward Alfred. *The Loyalists of New Jersey: Their Memorials, Petitions, Claims, Etc. from English Records*. New Jersey Historical Society, 1927.

Jones, Thomas. *History of New York During the Revolutionary War*. New York Historical Society, 1879.

Journal of Lancaster's Historical Society. Lancaster, Pennsylvania, 2019.

Kaplan, Sidney, and Emma Nogrady. *The Black Presence in the Era of the American Revolution*. University of Massachusetts, 1989.

Keelen, Kate, and Jerry Keelen. *The Navesink Watershed: A Brief History*. Navesink Swimming River Group, 2003.

King, John P. *Highlands New Jersey*. Arcadia Publishing, 2001.

Kirkpatrick, Trevor. *Loyalist Trails, 2007–22*. United Empire Loyalist Association of Canada, 2007.

Knight, Charles. *The Popular History of England: An Illustrated History of Society and Government from the Earliest Period to Our Own Times*. Vol. 7. Bradbury and Evans, 1861.

Konstam, Angus. *American Privateers of the Revolutionary War*. Bloomsbury Publishers, 2020.

Lawler, Andrew. "A Perfect Frenzy: A Royal Governor, His Black Allies, and the Crisis that Spurred the American Revolution." *Atlantic Monthly Press* (2025).

Leavitt, Delynn. *The Three Brothers: The Hendrickson Family of Middletown, New Jersey*. Henry Hendricks Family Organization, 2015.

Lender, Mark Edward, and Garry Wheeler Stone. *Fatal Sunday, George Washington, the Monmouth Campaign, and the Politics of Battle*. University of Oklahoma, 2016.

Lincoln, Charles H. *The Revolutionary Movement in Pennsylvania, 1760–1776*. University of Pennsylvania, 1901.

Lincoln, Charles Henry, ed. *Naval Records of the American Revolution*. Washington, D.C.: Government Printing Office, 1906.

Longstreet, Rubert James. "A Longstreet Family History." RootsWeb. https://sites.rootsweb.com/~longstrt/history.html.

Lossing, Benson J. *The Pictorial Field-Book of the Revolution*. Harper & Brothers, 1850.

Lossing, Benson J., ed. *The American Historical Record, and Repertory of Notes and Queries*. Vol. 2. Westminster Publishing, 1873.

Lundin, Leonard. *Cockpit of the Revolution: The War for Independence in New Jersey*. Lundn Press, 1940.

Lurie, Maxine N., and Richard F. Veit. *Envisioning New Jersey: An Illustrated History of the Garden State*. Rutgers University Press, 2016.

Lurie, Maxine, and Peter O. Wacker. *Mapping New Jersey: An Evolving Landscape*. Rivergate Books, 2009.

———. *New Jersey: A History of the Garden State*. Rutgers University Press, 2012.

Lurie, Maxine N., ed. *A New Jersey Anthology*. Rutgers University, 1994.

Lurie, Maxine N. *Taking Sides in Revolutionary New Jersey: Caught in the Crossfire*. Rutgers University, 2022.

MacKenzie, George Norbert, ed. *Colonial Families of the United States of America: In Which Is Given the History, Genealogy and Armorial Bearings of Colonial Families*. Seaford Press, 1917.

Marcus, Jacob Rader. *Memoirs of American Jews, 1775–1865*. Jewish Publication Society of America, 1955.

Martin, Dorothy L. *Revenge and Retribution: The Death of Philip White, New Jersey Loyalist*. United Empire Loyalist Association of Canada, 1998.

Matthews, Christopher N. *The Black Freedom Struggle in Northern New Jersey, 1613–1860: A Review of the Literature*. Montclair State University, 2019.

Mayo, Bernard, ed. *Jefferson Himself: The Personal Narrative of a Many-Sided American*. University Press of Virginia, 1942.

Meacham, John. *Thomas Jefferson: The Art of Power*. Random House, 2012.

Miller, Francis Trevelyan. *The Journal of American History*. Vol. 3. Associated Publishers of American Records Inc., 1909.

Miller, Pauline S. *Ocean County: Four Centuries in the Making*. Ocean County Cultural & Heritage Commission, 2000.

———. "200 Years Ago Tomorrow Patriot Hanged at Highlands." *Asbury Park Press*, April 11, 1982.

Mills, W. Jay. *Historic Houses of New Jersey*. J.B. Lippincott, 1903.

Mitnick, Barbara J., ed. *New Jersey in the American Revolution*. Rutgers University Press, 2005.

Monea, Nino C. "A Constitutional History of Debtors' Prisons." *Drexel Law Review* (2022).

Monmouth County Clerk Archives. Common Pleas. Manalapan, New Jersey.

Monmouth County Historical Association Archives. Coll. 72, Box 4, Series III. Freehold, New Jersey.

Monmouth County Historic Sites Inventory, updated January 2023.

Montgomery, Thomas Lynch, ed. *Pennsylvania Archives*. 5th series, vol. 1. Harrisburg Publishing Company, 1906.

Moody, James. *Narrative of the Exertions and Sufferings of Lieut. James Moody, in Cause of Government Since the Year 1776*. Private printing, 1782.

Moon, Robert Charles. *The Morris Family of Philadelphia, Descendants of Anthony Morris, 1654–1721*. Privately published, 1909.

Moore, Frank. *The Diary of the Revolution: A Centennial Volume Embracing the Current Events in Our County's History from 1775 to 1781*. J.B. Burr Publishers, 1876.

Morgan, William James, ed. *Naval Documents of the American Revolution*. Vol. 7. Naval Historical Center, 1976.

Morrissey, Brendan. *Monmouth Courthouse 1778: The Last Great Battle in the North*. Bloomsbury USA, 2004.

Murrin, Mary R. *New Jersey Historical Manuscripts: A Guide to Collections in the State*. New Jersey Historical Commission, 1978.

Mustin, M., ed. *A Sketch of Monmouth County, New Jersey, 1683–1929*. M. Mustin Company, 1929.

Mutter, J. Mark. *The Founding of Our Town and the Creation of Our County*. Toms River Township, 2010.

National Register of Historic Places Inventory Nomination Form. "Old Village of Toms River." National Park Service, 1982.

Neilson Family Papers. Box 10. Special Collections, Rutgers University.

Nelson, Craig. *Thomas Paine: Enlightenment, Revolution, and the Birth of Modern Nations*. Penguin, 2006.

Nelson, William, ed. *Documents Relating to the Colonial History of the State of New Jersey*. Vols. 25 and 27. Press Printing and Publishing Company, 1903 and 1905.

———. *Documents Relating to the Revolutionary History of the State of New Jersey*. Vol. 4. State Gazette Publishing, 1914.

———. *The New Jersey Coast in Three Centuries*. Lewis Publishing, 1902.

———. *New Jersey Marriage Records, 1650–1800*. Press Printing & Publishing, 1900.

New Jersey General Assembly. *Journals of the Legislative Council of the State of New Jersey, October 3, 1776*. Isaac Collins, 1776.

New Jersey Historical Society. Proceedings, 1925.

New Jersey Historic Preservation Office. Monmouth County Historic Sites Inventory Summary Report, 1984.

New Jersey Legislature. "Selections from the Correspondence of the Executive of New Jersey from 1776 to 1786." *Newark Daily Advertiser*, 1848.

New Jersey Society of Pennsylvania. *Decennial Record, 1907–1917*. New Jersey Society of Pennsylvania, 1919.

New Jersey State Archives, Trenton, New Jersey.

New Shrewsbury Tercentenary Committee. *Historical Scrapbook of the Borough of New Shrewsbury, New Jersey*. 1964.

Northrup, Henry Davenport. *The Student's History of the United States, from the Discovery of the American Continent to the Present Time*. New England Home-Educational Society, 1901.

Ocean County Historical Society. *Along the Toms River*. Arcadia Publishing, 1996.

Ocean County Principals' Council. *Tides of Time: A History of Ocean County, New Jersey, Written by School Pupils*. C.E. Howe & Company, 1940.

Oliver, Edmund. *Cassell's History of the United States*. Cassell, Petter & Galpin, 1874.

Olsen, Judith M. Lippincott. *5 Generations of the Descendants of Richard and Abigail Lippincott*. Gloucester County Historical Society, 1982.

Paine, Thomas. *The American Crisis and Letter to Sir Guy Carleton, on the Murder of Captain Huddy, and the Intended Retaliation on Captain Asgill of the Guards*. Daniel Isaac Eaton, 1788.

Palfreyman, Brett. "The Story Behind the Story: Telling the History of Colonel Tye at Sandy Hook." *New Jersey Studies*. Rutgers University. https://njs.libraries.rutgers.edu/index.php/njs/article/view/336.

Papas, Phillip. *That Ever Loyal Island: Staten Island and the American Revolution*. New York University Press, 2007.

Pattee, Fred Lewis. *Poems of Philip Freneau, Poet of the American Revolution*. Princeton Historical Society, 1907.

Pavlac, Brian A. "Marie Antoinette, Queen of France." King's College. https://departments.kings.edu/womens_history/marieantoi.html.

Pearson, Michael. *Those Damned Rebels: The American Revolution as Seen Through British Eyes*. Da Capo Press, 1972.

Pennsylvania Packet. October 3, 1780.

Pepe, Barbara. *Freehold: A Hometown History*. Arcadia Publishing, 2003.

Perkins, James Breck. *France in the American Revolution*. Houghton Mifflin Company, 1911.

Pettit, Augusta A. *Some Genealogical Notes on the Borden, Lloyd, Levis Families of Shrewsbury, East Jersey and Salem County, New Jersey*. Privately printed, 1932.

Pfister, Jude M. "John Dickinson and His Letters." *Journal of the American Revolution* (April 2024).

Philadelphia Gazette. November 22, 1775, and September 9, 1780.

Pierce, Arthur Dudley. *Smugglers' Woods: Jaunts and Journeys in Colonial and Revolutionary New Jersey*. Rutgers University Press, 1960.

Pine, Alan S., Jean C. Hershenov and Aaron H. Lefkowitz. *Peddler to Suburbanite: The History of the Jews of Monmouth County, New Jersey: From the Colonial Period to 1980*. Monmouth Jewish Community Council, 1981.

Pingeon, Frances D. *Blacks in the Revolutionary Era*. New Jersey Historical Commission, 1975.

Preston, Antony, David Lyon and John H. Batchelor. *Navies of the American Revolution*. Prentice-Hall, 1975.

Price, David. *Winning the Ten Crucial Days: The Keys to Victory in George Washington's Legendary Winter Campaign*. Brookline Books, 2025.

Proceedings of the Bostonian Society at the Annual Meeting, January 10, 1893.

Proceedings of the New Jersey Historical Society: A Magazine of History, Biography and Genealogy 2 (1917).

Provincial Archives of New Brunswick, Canada. "Court Martial of Capt. Richard Lippincott, 1782." https://archives.gnb.ca/archives/?culture=en-CA.

Prowell, George R. *History of Camden County, New Jersey*. L.J. Richards & Company, 1886.

Publications of the Genealogical Society of Pennsylvania 6 (1917).

Pulis, John W., ed. *Moving On: Black Loyalists in the Afro-Atlantic World*. Garland Publishing, 1999.

Quarles, Benjamin. "Lord Dunmore as Liberator." *William and Mary Quarterly* (October 1958).

———. *The Negro in the American Revolution*. University of North Carolina Press, 1961.

Randall, Willard S. *The Proprietary House in Amboy*. Proprietary House Association, 1975.

Raser, Edward J. "American Prisoners Taken at the Battle of Navesink, 1777." *Genealogical Magazine of New Jersey* (May 1970).

Raum, John O. *The History of New Jersey from Its Earliest Settlement to the Present Time*. Vol. 2. John E. Potter and Company, 1877.

Reef, Catherine. *A to Z of African Americans: African Americans in the Military*. Infobase Publishing, 2010.

Rees, John U. "'Negro, Mulatto, or Indian Man Slave[s]': African Americans in the Rhode Island Regiments, 1775–1783." American Battlefield Trust, 2024.

———. *They Were Good Soldiers: African-Americans Serving in the Continental Army, 1775–1783*. Helion Limited, 2019.

———. "'What Is This You Have Been About To Day?': The New Jersey Brigade at the Battle of Monmouth." RevWar '75. https://revwar75.com/library/rees/monmouth/MonmouthToc.htm.

Rees, John U., and Don Troiani. *Don Troiani's Black Soldiers in America's Wars, 1754–1865*. Globe Pequot/Stackpole Books, 2025.

Regimental Nicknames and Traditions of the British Army. 5th ed. Gale & Polden, 1916.

Reid, Juliet Prowse, and Simon Fowler. *Genealogical Research in England's Public Record Office: A Guide for North Americans*. 2nd ed. Genealogical Publishing Company, 1996.

Renehan, Edward J. *The Treaty of Paris: The Precursor to a New Nation*. Infobase Publishing, 2007.

Richard Grubb & Associates Inc. *The Garden State Parkway*. 2000.

Richmond, Reverend J.F. *New York and Its Institutions, 1609–1872*. E.B. Treat, 1872.

RootsWeb. "Toms River, Ocean, New Jersey." https://freepages.rootsweb.com/~tolleygenealogy/genealogy/tomsriver.html.

Rumson Board of Education. *History of Rumson, 1665–1944*. Schuyler Press, 1944.

Ruset, Ben. "The Jersey Taverns." NJ Pine Barrens, 2011. NJPineBarrens.com.

Ryan, Dennis P. *New Jersey in the American Revolution, 1763–1783: A Chronology*. New Jersey Historical Commission, 1943.

———. *New Jersey's Loyalists*. New Jersey Historical Commission, 1975.

———. *Six Towns: Continuity and Change in Revolutionary New Jersey, 1770–1792*. New York University, 1974.

Ryerson, Egerton. *The Loyalists of America and Their Times from 1620 to 1816*. Vol. 2. Dawson Brothers, 1880.

Salem County Historical Society. "Place Names of Salem County, N.J." 1964.

———. "Salem County in the Revolution." 1967.

Salerno, Anthony. "The Social Background of Seventeenth-Century Emigration to America." *Journal of British Studies* 19, no. 1 (Autumn 1979).

Salter, Edwin. "Historical Reminiscences of Ocean County, New Jersey." *New Jersey Courier*, 1878.

———. "Historical Sketches." *New Jersey Courier*, 1866.

———. *A History of Monmouth and Ocean Counties: Embracing a Genealogical Record of Earliest Settlers in Monmouth and Their Descendants*. Gardner & Son, Publishers, 1890.

———. "Huguenot Settlers and Land Owners in Monmouth County, New Jersey." *New York Genealogical and Biographical Record*, 1889.

Salter, Edwin, and George C. Beekman. *Old Times in Old Monmouth: Historical Reminiscences of Old Monmouth County, New Jersey, Being a Series of Historical Sketches Relating to Old Monmouth County*. Y.S. Yard, 1887.

Sanborn Maps of New Jersey. Freehold, New Jersey.

Saretzky, Gary D., ed. "Buildings in Monmouth: Stories and Styles." Catalogue of the exhibition at the Monmouth County Library. Manalapan, New Jersey, October 2018. https://www.monmouthcountyclerk.com/wp-content/uploads/2018/10/Catalog-Buildings-exhibit-v3-reduced.pdf.

———. "Celebrating New Jersey's Archives: Documents of the American Revolution." Monmouth County Archives, 2002. https://www.monmouthcountyclerk.com/wp-content/uploads/2017/04/2002-Catalog-Revolution.pdf.

———. "Documents of the American Revolution: Joshua Huddy Era." Catalogue of the exhibition at the Monmouth County Library, Manalapan, New Jersey, 2004. https://www.monmouthcountyclerk.com/wp-content/uploads/2017/04/2004-Catalog-Am-Rev-Huddy.pdf.

———. "Documents of the American Revolution: William Livingston." Catalogue of the exhibition at the Monmouth County Library, Manalapan, New Jersey, 2003. https://www.monmouthcountyclerk.com/wp-content/uploads/2017/04/2003-Catalog-Am-Rev-Livingtson.pdf.

Savage, James. *A Genealogical Dictionary of the First Settlers of New England Showing Three Generations of Those Who Came Before May, 1692, on the Basis of Farmer's Register*. Little, Brown and Company, 1860.

Schenck, Alexander Du Bois. *The Rev. William Schenck, His Ancestry and His Descendants*. Rufus Darby, 1883.

Schneider, John. *A Historical Journey Across Raritan Bay*. The History Press, 2020.

Scots Magazine (1782). Murray and Cochrane.

Sheffer, Debra J. *The Buffalo Soldiers, Their Epic Story and Major Campaigns*. Praeger, 2015.

Sherwin, W.T. *Memoirs of the Life of Thomas Paine with Observations on His Writings*. R. Carlile, 1819.

Shomette, Donald Grady. *Privateers of the Revolution: War on the New Jersey Coast, 1775–1783*. Schiffer Publishing, 2016.

Showman, Richard K., ed. *The Papers of General Nathanael Greene*. Vol. 5. North Carolina University Press, 1989.

Sickler, Joseph S. *The History of Salem County New Jersey, Being the Story of John Fenwick's Colony*. Sunbeam Publishing, 1937.

Simcoe, John Graves. *A Journal of the Operations of the Queen's Rangers, from the End of the Year 1777 to the Conclusion of the Late American War*. Privately printed, 1787.

Sinnott, Mary Elizabeth. *Annals of the Sinnott, Rogers, Coffin, Corlies, Reeves, Bodine and Allied Families*. J.B. Lippincott Company, 1905.

Skemp, Sheila L. *William Franklin: Son of a Patriot, Servant of a King*. Oxford University Press, 1990.

Smith, James M. "Thomas Hutchinson, Patrick Henry, and the Stamp Act." *Journal of the American Revolution* (August 2024).

Snyder, John P. *The Story of New Jersey's Civil Boundaries, 1606–1698*. New Jersey Bureau of Genealogy and Topography, 1969.

Society of Colonial Wars in the State of New Jersey. "Historic Roadsides in New Jersey." 1928.

Soderlund, Jean R. *Lenape Country: Delaware Valley Society Before William Penn*. University of Pennsylvania Press, 2015.

———. *Separate Paths: Lenapes and Colonists in West New Jersey*. Rutgers University Press, 2022.

Sparks, Jared. *The Writings of George Washington*. Little, Brown, & Company, 1855.

Spirit of '76. "Captain Huddy and the Fall of the North Ministry" (1898).

Stahr, Walter. *John Jay, Founding Father*. Diversion Publishing Corporation, 2012.

State of Pennsylvania. *Minutes of the Supreme Executive Council of Pennsylvania. Vol. 12*. Theo Fenn & Company, 1853.

Stellhorn, Paul A., and Michael J. Birkner, eds. *The Governors of New Jersey, 1664–1974: Biographical Essays*. New Jersey Historical Commission, 1982.

Stewart, Frank H. "Salem More than a Century Ago, Extracts from the 'Salem Messenger' from September, 1819, to December, 1822." Reprinted from the *Salem Standard and Jerseyman*, 1935.

Stillwell, Dr. John E. *Historical and Genealogical Miscellany: Data Relating to the Settlement and Settlers of New York and New Jersey*. Vols. 1–5. Privately published, 1903–32.

Stone, William L. *The Centennial History of New York City from the Discovery to the Present Day*. R.D. Cooke, 1876.

Stouck, David. *The Wardells and Vosburghs: Records of a Loyalist Family*. Privately printed, 1986.

Stratton, Harriet Russell. *A Book of Strattons*. Vol. 1, *Being a Collection of Stratton Records from England and Scotland, and a Genealogical History of the Early Colonial Strattons in America, with Five Generations of Their Descendants*. Grafton Press, 1908.

Stryker, William S. *The Capture of the Block House at Toms River, New Jersey, March 24, 1782*. Naar, Day, & Naar, 1883.

———. *"The New Jersey Volunteers" (Loyalists) in the Revolutionary War*. Naar, Day, & Naar, 1887.

———. *Official Register of the Officers and Men in the Revolutionary War*. Wm. T. Nicholson & Company, 1872.

Symmes, Reverend Frank R. *History of the Old Tennent Church with Biographical Sketches of Its Pastors*. James S. Yard & Son, 1897.

Tanner, Edwin P. "The Province of New Jersey, 1664–1738." Thesis, Columbia University, 1908.

Tappert, Theodore G., and John W. Doberstein, eds. *The Journals of Henry Melchior Muhlenberg, in Three Volumes*. Muhlenberg Press, 1958.

Thompson, Elizabeth Makin. *Colts Neck Old Homes and Families*. Privately printed, 1987.

Thompson, William Y. *Israel Shreve, Revolutionary War Officer*. McGinty Publications, 1979.

Tomlinson, Everitt T. *The Boys of Old Monmouth, a Story of Washington's Campaign in New Jersey in 1778*. Houghton, Mifflin, 1898.

Union Landing Historical Society. *Brielle, New Jersey: Saltworks to Suburb*. The History Press, 2009.

Upper Freehold Better Township Association. *Upper Freehold Township: A Survey of the Life, Resources and Government of a New Jersey Rural Township, with a Program for Improvement*. New Jersey Department of Agriculture, 1935.

Walling, Richard S. *Men of Color at the Battle of Monmouth, June 28, 1778: The Role of African Americans and Native Americans at Monmouth: Containing a Brief History of These Men of Color and a Presentation of Nearly Two Hundred Names and Identifications*. Longstreet House, 1994.

Walsh, Maya. *Captain Joshua Huddy: The Hero Martyr of Monmouth*. Historical Society of Highlands, 1997.

Ward, Matthew H. "Joshua Huddy: The Scourge of New Jersey Loyalists." *Journal of the American Revolution* (2018).

Weeks, Daniel J. *Not for Filthy Lucre's Sake: Richard Saltar and the Antiproprietary Movement in East New Jersey, 1665–1707*. Associated University Presses, 2001.

Weiss, Harry B., and Grace M. Weiss. *The Revolutionary Saltworks of the New Jersey Coast*. Past Times Press, 1959.

Werther, Richard J. "The Plot to Partition America." All Things Liberty, February 2025. https://allthingsliberty.com/2025/02/the-plot-to-partition-america.

Westcote, Thomas. *A View of Devonshire in MDCXXX, with a Pedigree of Most of Its Gentry*. William Roberts, 1845.

Whalen, William J. *What Quakers Believe*. Friends General Conference, 1982.

White, James Edward. *A Genealogical History of the Descendants of Peter White, of New Jersey, from 1670, and of William White and Deborah Tilton His Wife, Loyalists*. Barnes & Company, 1906.

White, William. *History, Gazetteer, and Directory of Devonshire and the City and County of Exeter*. Robert Leader, 1850.

Wickersty, Jason R. "Were There Really 1,500 British Wagons on the Road to Monmouth?" *Journal of the American Revolution* (July 2024).

Wieczorek, Scott. *The Tale of Ocean County Salt*. Ocean County Historical Society Scroll, 2002.

Wiggins, E. Stone. *The History of Queen's County, New Brunswick*. Watchman, 1877.

Willard, Margaret Wheeler. *Letters on the American Revolution, 1774–1776*. Houghton Mifflin, 1925.

Williams, Henry Llewellyn, and Jeremy Belknap. *The Two Americas: Their Complete History, from the Earliest Discoveries to the Present Day*. Will. C. Sadlier, 1881.

Wilson, Thomas B. *Notices from New Jersey Newspapers, 1781–1790*. Hunterdon House, 1988.

Winsor, Justin. *Narrative and Critical History of America*. Vol. 6. Houghton, Mifflin and Company, 1887.

Women's Project of New Jersey Inc. *Past and Promise: Lives of New Jersey Women*. Syracuse University Press, 1997.

Woodhull, Alfred Alexander. *Address at the Annual Meeting, New Jersey Society of Pennsylvania*. Philadelphia, PA, 1914.

Woodward, Major E.M., and John F. Hageman. *History of Burlington and Mercer Counties, New Jersey with Biographical Sketches*. Everts & Peck, 1883.

Wright, Esther Clark. *The Loyalists of New Brunswick*. Lancelot Press, 1977.

Wright, Waldo Carlton. "The Captain Asgill Affair." *Dalhousie Review* 42, no. 4 (1963).

Wroblewski, Joseph E. "Colonel Tye: Leader of Loyalist Raiders and Runaway Slave." *Journal of the American Revolution* (February 17, 2021).

———. "The War Years (1775–1783)." *Journal of the American Revolution* (June 2021).

Wyoming Historical and Geological Society. *Proceedings and Collections for the Year 1901*. 1902.

Zielinski, Adam E. *Life in Colonial America Prior to the Revolutionary War*. American Battlefield Trust, 2020.

Zimmerman, Colin. "Burlington 1776: The Forgotten Opportunity." *Journal of the American Revolution* (2023).

INDEX

D

E

F

G

H

Q

R

S

W

Y

ABOUT THE AUTHOR

Monmouth County Clerk's Office.

Rick Geffken has authored numerous articles on New Jersey history and presented historical papers at the New Jersey History & Historic Preservation, the New Jersey Education Association, the New Jersey Library Association and the Institute for Advanced Study (Princeton). This is Rick Geffken's fourth book for Arcadia Publishing/The History Press. He's part of the New Jersey Slavery Records Index project under the auspices of Rutgers University (New Brunswick, New Jersey). He joined the New Jersey Social Justice Reconciliation Committee to commemorate the only recorded lynching of a Black man in New Jersey.

In 2023, Rick was recognized for his historical contributions by the Monmouth County Historical Association and the Monmouth County Clerk for his efforts in the preservation and knowledge of Monmouth County history.

A former U.S. Army officer and Vietnam veteran, Rick retired from a career with Hewlett-Packard. He earned a BS from St. Peter's University, a Teaching Certificate from Monmouth University and an MA from Montclair State University.

Rick is a trustee of the Shrewsbury Historical Society. He formerly served on the board of the Friends of Cedar View Cemetery and the Jersey Coast Heritage Museum at Sandlass House. He is a current board member of Truehart Productions and an advisor to the Tinton Falls Historic Preservation Commission, the Board of the Asbury Park Museum and the Monmouth County Historical Association.

For a list of Rick's presentation topics, see https://www.gardenstatelegacy.com/GSL_Speakers_Bureau.html. For detailed information on his speaking engagements, please contact rickg0817@yahoo.com.